THE

RED RIVER EXPEDITION.

ROUTE
of the
RED RIVER EXPEDITIONARY FORCE
from
TORONTO TO FORT GARRY

The figures represent the distances in Miles from
Toronto.

THE

RED RIVER
EXPEDITION

CAPTAIN G. L. HUYSHE,
RIFLE BRIGADE
LATE ON THE STAFF OF COLONEL SIR GARNETT WOLSELEY

The Naval & Military Press Ltd

published in association with

FIREPOWER
The Royal Artillery Museum
Woolwich

Published by
The Naval & Military Press Ltd
Unit 10 Ridgewood Industrial Park,
Uckfield, East Sussex,
TN22 5QE England
Tel: +44 (0) 1825 749494
Fax: +44 (0) 1825 765701
www.naval-military-press.com

in association with

FIREPOWER
The Royal Artillery Museum, Woolwich
www.firepower.org.uk

The Naval & Military
Press

MILITARY HISTORY AT YOUR
FINGERTIPS

... a unique and expanding series of reference works

Working in collaboration with the foremost
regiments and institutions, as well as acknowledged
experts in their field, N&MP have assembled a
formidable array of titles including technologically
advanced CD-ROMs and facsimile reprints of
impossible-to-find rarities.

TO

COLONEL SIR GARNET WOLSELEY, C.B., K.C.M.G

TO WHOSE SKILL AND ENERGY

THE SUCCESS OF THE RED RIVER EXPEDITION WAS MAINLY DUE

THESE PAGES ARE RESPECTFULLY

𝔇𝔢𝔡𝔦𝔠𝔞𝔱𝔢𝔡.

PREFACE.

THE following brief account of the Red River Expedition has been mainly put together from the everyday jottings of a private journal, and lays no claim to any literary merit. It has been written in the hope of directing attention to the successful accomplishment of an expedition which was attended with more than ordinary difficulties, but which was completely overshadowed from first to last by the absorbing interest of a great Continental war.

Through the kindness of Sir Garnet Wolseley, I have had access to the official documents of the Expedition; I have also availed myself of the Reports on the line of route published by Mr. Dawson, C.E., and by the Topographical Department of the War Office. The statements made may therefore, I hope, be relied on as

accurate and impartial. My aim has been to
" extenuate naught, nor set down aught in malice."
Political questions have been avoided as much
as the nature of the subject would permit, as
I feel that they do not come within the province
of a soldier.

I have endeavoured to avoid tiring the general
reader with dry details of military movements,
and yet not to sacrifice the character of the work
as an account of a military expedition. Whether
or not between these two stools I have fallen
to the ground, I must leave to the judgment of
a kind and generous public, only premising that,
as the book is not very voluminous, I trust
I have not trespassed too much on their for-
bearance.

G. L. H.

Woolwich,
March 20th, 1871.

CONTENTS.

APPENDICES.

LIST OF MAPS AND ILLUSTRATIONS.

* *Printed, by permission, from the Journal of the R.U.S. Institution.*

NARRATIVE

RED RIVER EXPEDITION, &c.

CHAPTER I.

INTRODUCTORY.—THE RED RIVER SETTLEMENT.

VERY near the centre of the northern or British portion of the vast continent of North America, and almost equally unapproachable from north, south, east or west, is a small settlement, the very existence of which was hardly known to the outside world until within the last few months.

Founded in 1813 by Alexander Lord Selkirk, who obtained from the Hudson's Bay Company a grant of land near the confluence of the Assiniboine and Red rivers, this little colony was at first known by the name of its founder, but latterly has received the general appellation of the Red River Settlement. For many years it

B

had a precarious existence, having been several times threatened with extinction, both from its Indian neighbours and also from a still more formidable enemy, the plague of locusts or grasshoppers. It also suffered severely from the quarrels of the Hudson's Bay and North-West Companies until the amalgamation of the two rival trading Companies in 1822.

The situation chosen by Lord Selkirk for his Scotch emigrants was however so favourable, and the natural fertility of the soil so great, that the infant colony successfully struggled through these difficulties, and, receiving constant accessions to its strength, spread itself along the banks of both rivers till it attained the respectable population of about 15,000 souls.

Upon the completion of the great Act of Confederation of the British North American Provinces in 1867, the attention of Canadian statesmen was turned to this distant land, and negotiations were opened for the transfer of the North-West Territory to the new Dominion of Canada. The age of monopolies was past. The resumption by the Crown of its great Indian Empire in 1858, and the consequent extinction of the East India Company, had paved the way for a similar resumption of the vast tract of land granted by royal charter in King Charles the Second's time to "The Governor and Company of Adventurers of England trading into Hudson's Bay." The transfer was to be a kind of triangular arrangement. All territorial rights claimed by the Hudson's Bay Company were to be annulled on payment of 300,000*l.* by Canada, and the country would then be handed over by royal proclamation to the Dominion Government, the Company being only allowed to retain a certain amount of land in the vicinity of its trading posts.

The transfer was fixed for the 1st December, 1869; but the Dominion Cabinet, eager to secure the rich prize, and at the same time perhaps not sorry to get rid of a somewhat intractable servant, appointed its Minister of Public Works, the Honourable William McDougall, C.B., to be the Lieutenant-Governor of the North-West Territories, and sent him off in the month of September with instructions to proceed to Fort Garry "with all convenient speed," there to assist the formal transfer of the Territories, and to be "ready to assume the government" as soon as the transfer was completed.

In these negotiations between the Hudson's Bay

Company and the Imperial and Dominion Govern-
ments, it does not appear that the feelings of the
little colony at Red River were taken into account
at all. The French Emperor had not then set the
world the example of a *plebiscite* vote; the con-
currence of the people so vitally interested does not
appear to have been asked, nor was any guarantee
that their rights and privileges should be respected
held out as an inducement to the settlers to ac-
quiesce quietly in the new order of things. Though
there can be no doubt that they would have been
fairly and justly treated by Canada, yet it cannot
be a matter of wonder to any impartial person
that they did not take quite the same view of
the matter, but objected to be transformed from
a Crown colony to a "colony of a colony," and
handed over to the Dominion, *bon gré mal gré*,
like so many head of cattle.

During the summer of 1869, a surveying party
under a Colonel Dennis, of Volunteer fame, had
been engaged surveying the country and dividing
it into townships, &c., for future allotment by the
Canadian Government. The proceedings of this
party had given great offence to the French half-
breeds. The unsettled state of the land tenure as
regards the half-breeds and Indians not unnaturally

excited apprehensions in their minds that their
lands would be taken from them and given to
Canadian immigrants ; and the injudicious conduct
of some of the members of the surveying party,
who put up claims here and there to tracts of
land that they happened to take a fancy to, did
not tend to allay these angry feelings. The irritation raised by these causes operating together on
the uneducated French half-breeds culminated on
the 10th October, 1869, in open opposition to the
surveying party : a band of some eighteen men,
headed by a man named Louis Riel, stopped one
of Colonel Dennis's surveying parties, and compelled them to discontinue their operations. Governor McTavish, then senior officer of the Hudson's
Bay Company, and therefore the governor of the
settlement, was appealed to in vain : Riel refused
to allow the survey to continue, declaring that
the Canadian Government had no right to survey
the lands that belonged to the French settlers.
The party was accordingly withdrawn, and, en-
couraged by this first success, the disaffected
French resolved to prevent the entry of Mr.
McDougall into the Territory. They formed themselves into a Provisional Government, electing
a man named John Bruce, a French half-breed,

as president, and Louis Riel as secretary. The latter, however, was the ruling spirit, and exercised the real power, and very shortly after assumed himself the title of president.

The new "Provisional Government" proceeded to act with energy; a small armed force was established on Scratching River, about fifteen miles from Fort Garry, and a barricade thrown up across the road leading to Pembina; a messenger bearing the following letter was also despatched to the boundary line to await the arrival of Mr. McDougall :—

Datée à St. Norbert, Rivière Rouge,
ce 21*ème Jour d'Octobre*, 1869.

Monsieur,

   Le Comité National des Metis de la Rivière Rouge intime à M. Wm. McDougall l'ordre de ne pas entrer sur le territoire du Nord-Ouest sans une permission spéciale de ce Comité.

Par ordre du Président John Bruce,

Louis Riel, Secrétaire.

A Monsieur McDougall.

This letter was handed to Mr. McDougall by the bearer, a French half-breed, on the 30th October, upon his arrival at the American Custom-house at Pembina, sixty miles from Fort Garry, and on the border line between British and American territory.

"PRESIDENT" LOUIS RIEL.

To face p. 6.

He took no notice of it, but continued his journey two miles further to the Hudson's Bay Company's post, *inside* the North-West Territory.

Three days afterwards, namely on the evening of the 2nd November, an armed party of fourteen horsemen approached from the direction of Fort Garry, and, dismounting at the gate of the stockade which surrounds the post, sent in two of their number, who politely but firmly intimated to Mr. McDougall that, by order of the Provisional Government, he must leave the North-West Territory by nine o'clock the following morning. This order was peremptorily enforced, and the Lieutenant-Governor Designate of the North-West Territory was ignominiously expelled by an armed force of French half-breeds from the land he had come to rule.

During the month of November Mr. McDougall remained quietly at Pembina, keeping up an occasional correspondence with Governor McTavish and the well-disposed inhabitants of the settlement, and waiting for the opportunity, which never came, of entering the Territory. The English and Scotch settlers, though favourably disposed to Canada, were yet unwilling, either from lack

of energy or from fear of commencing a civil
strife, to compromise themselves openly in Mr.
McDougall's favour, and allowed things to take
their own course.

On the 24th November, Riel, with an armed
party, took possession of Fort Garry, ostensibly
to prevent its falling into the hands of Mr.
McDougall, but in reality to obtain funds and
provisions for carrying out his plan of making
himself sole ruler of the country. Governor
McTavish had twelve hours' notice of the intended occupation of the fort, but took no
measures to prevent it. And here I must ob-
serve, that the uniform success of the insurgents
in all their plans points undoubtedly, not only
to advice and assistance from their own clergy
(which is too notorious to need any argument),
but also to sympathy, if not collusion, on the
part of some of the Hudson's Bay Company's
officials at Fort Garry. It is impossible to acquit
the latter of all blame. Their utter inertness,
and *laissez aller* policy, cannot be explained
away by the illness of the Governor. He had
the advice of a council, composed of many of
the leading residents, to whom the prevalent
feeling of discontent must have been well known,

but yet nothing was done to check the rising spirit of rebellion, which soon passed beyond the control of its originators. Nothing could have been easier than to have prevented Riel's occupation of the fort by simply shutting the gates and refusing to let him in. Without the fort and its stores of money, arms, ammunition, and provisions, the *émeute* must have fallen to the ground of itself, and have collapsed for want of the necessaries of life. The only rational inference can be, that the Company's officials at Fort Garry were secretly pleased to find that Canada was not going to have such an easy time of it as she expected, and, loth to lose the government of the country themselves, they looked on with indifference at the troubles which welcomed their successors. Any danger to themselves they did not anticipate. Their eyes were blinded so that they could not see. When too late, they found out the error into which they had been betrayed. They found a despotic ruler established for nine months in their own fort, feeding his men on the Company's provisions, and paying them with the Company's money. Dearly indeed did they pay for their shortsightedness!

It was, however, only amongst the Company's

officials at Fort Garry itself that this unfortunate sympathy with the rebels existed. Elsewhere their loyalty was above suspicion, and the assistance they rendered to the expeditionary force during the next summer along the whole line of route was invaluable, and will be gladly acknowledged by every member of the expedition.

The 1st of December had been the day fixed for the transfer of the territory to Canada; accordingly, towards midnight on the 30th November, Mr. McDougall and his party sallied forth from their residence at Pembina, crossed the frontier, and took formal possession of the North-West Territory in the name of the Canadian Government. The cold was intense, the thermometer standing at 20° below zero, consequently there was no one to oppose this valorous but somewhat ludicrous proceeding. But the next act of Mr. McDougall was, unfortunately, not so ludicrous, and might have been attended with the most unhappy consequences. He issued two proclamations to the inhabitants of Red River,—one, on the 1st December, announcing his appointment as Lieutenant-Governor from that day; the other, on the 2nd December, confirming all public functionaries in their present offices, except, of course,

Governor McTavish ; and lastly, he gave Colonel
Dennis a commission to act as Lieutenant and
Conservator of the Peace, and empowered him
to raise a body of armed men to put down the
insurrection by force.

Acting upon this commission, Colonel Dennis
proceeded to organize and drill the English and
Scotch settlers, took possession of the Stone Fort
(the Hudson's Bay Company's post twenty miles
below Fort Garry), and garrisoned it with fifty of
the loyal Indians from the Lower Settlement. A
collision between the two parties was now imminent ;
but fortunately, at this juncture, the urgent repre-
sentations of the English bishop and clergy, added
to a change in the feelings of the settlers produced
by the publication by the insurgents of a " Bill of
Rights," [1] induced Colonel Dennis to give up his
rash attempt, and on the 9th December he
ordered the loyal people to lay down their arms,
which indeed most of them had already done.

This attempt to resort to force had the effect
of strengthening the position of Riel in Fort
Garry ; aided by the influence and co-operation
of his active allies, the Roman Catholic clergy,
he managed to collect 400 or 500 men, whom he

[1] See Appendix A.

armed, clothed, fed, and paid from the plundering of the Hudson's Bay Company's stores, and from that time forth remained master of the situation.

Soon after these events Mr. McDougall, finding that he could do nothing to facilitate his entry into Fort Garry, returned to Canada, to meet there a storm of disapproval and censure from all sides, such as want of success seldom fails to elicit. The Canadian Cabinet condemned his policy in strong terms, and public opinion tried to make him the scapegoat for the blunders of others as well as for his own; but a calm and dispassionate review of the whole of the circumstances fails to endorse this wholesale condemnation.

Though he was at Pembina for a whole month before the 1st of December, yet he never received any intimation that the date of the transfer of the North-West Territory had been postponed. His position was a most embarrassing one. The loyal people of the settlement called upon him for some exposition of the state of affairs; therefore, assuming (as he had every right to do) that the date originally fixed for the transfer would not be altered without his being informed of it, he issued his Proclamation. Of his commission to Colonel Dennis, and his attempt to put down the insurrection by force

through that officer's assistance, the less said
perhaps the better. But it is curious to notice,
that whilst the Government fully approved of all
his acts up to the 1st December, yet after that
unfortunate Proclamation he was overwhelmed
with blame even for previous acts, to such an
extent that even his personal bearing and
manners did not escape the general censure.
Perhaps some of his greatest political enemies
and detractors might have fared no better, had
they been in his place.

In the meantime, intent on conciliatory measures,
the Ottawa Government sent two Commissioners,
Vicar-General Thiebault and Colonel de Salaberry,
to Red River. Mr. Donald Smith, the principal
officer of the Hudson's Bay Company in Canada,
was also sent a few days afterwards as a Special
Commissioner to inquire into and report on the
causes of the disturbances, and also to assist
Governor McTavish or relieve him of his duties,
should he be incapacitated by illness. Mr. Donald
Smith arrived at the Settlement on the 27th
December, was admitted into the fort, and obtained an interview with "President" Riel and
his council, the result of which was that he found
himself virtually a prisoner within the walls of the

fort. At this time there were some sixty British subjects held in close confinement as "political prisoners;" the British ensign had been hauled down, and in its place the flag of the "Provisional Government" (fleurs-de-lys and shamrocks) waved over Fort Garry; it was also the avowed determination of some of the leaders of the rebellion to bring about the annexation of the Territory to the United States. After much delay and opposition, Mr. Donald Smith was allowed to explain to the people the views of the Canadian Government at a mass meeting attended by upwards of 1,000 people, held on the 19th and 20th January, 1870, in the *open air*, notwithstanding the intense cold of the weather, 25 deg. *below* zero. The result of this meeting was the appointment of forty delegates, who met on the 25th January, and continued in consultation till February 10th. They finally decided on sending three delegates to Canada, and selected for that purpose Judge Black, the Rev. Father Richot, and Mr. Alfred H. Scott. A "Bill of Rights" was also prepared for submission to the Canadian Government.

During the sitting of the Convention, Riel broke out into open violence; he placed a guard

over Governor McTavish, who was then dangerously ill, and declared that he would have him
shot before midnight. He also seized Dr. Cowan,
the Hudson's Bay officer in charge of the district,
loaded him with abuse, and put him into confinement along with the other prisoners, threatening to shoot him within three hours if he did
not swear allegiance to the Provisional Government. His violence, however, soon cooled down;
and he released them on the 10th of February, and
on the 11th and 12th also set at liberty six or
eight of the other prisoners, and promised that the
remainder should also soon be released.

This improved condition of affairs did not, however, last long. The people at Prairie Portage (a
settlement about sixty miles from Fort Garry), being
determined to effect the release of the prisoners,
assembled to the number of 80 or 100, and were
joined by some 300 English and Scotch half-breeds.
The party was under the command of a Major
Boulton, formerly a captain in the 100th Regiment, and who had joined them much against
his own judgment, after striving ineffectually to
dissuade them from the attempt. They were un-
organized, undrilled, badly armed, and without
provisions, and utterly unable to cope with the

French party, who far exceeded them in numbers, and had large supplies of food, arms, and ammunition. Major Boulton's intention was to make a dash at the fort by night and carry it by a *coup de main;* but this plan, which indeed was the only one at all likely to be successful, was frustrated by a violent snow-storm on the very night on which the attempt was made. The road was rendered impassable by snow, and the party were unable to reach the fort before daylight. Their design thus got wind, and finding it now impossible to surprise the fort, they began to disperse to their homes. This action was quickened by inability to procure food for so large a number of men, and also by intelligence of the promised release of the prisoners, to effect which had been their main object in taking up arms.

On their way back to the Portage, forty-seven of them, including Major Boulton and one Thomas Scott, passed too near Fort Garry, and were captured by Riel on the 17th February. Boulton was tried by court-martial, and condemned to be shot at noon on the 18th; but at the urgent intercession of some of the most influential people in the settlement, his execution was postponed till midnight on the 19th. Poor Boulton, condemned to

a miserable and ignominious death at the hands
of a political faction, was kept in this dreadful
state of suspense until 11 P.M. on the 19th; he
had received the last sacrament from Archdeacon
McLean, had given his last commands, and having
lost all hopes of life, had prepared himself for death,
when, literally at the eleventh hour, Riel yielded to
the incessant solicitations of Mr. Donald Smith, and
pardoned him. It is difficult to imagine the revulsion
of feeling that he must have experienced when the
Archdeacon brought him the news of his pardon.

On the 26th February the elections were held
in the English parishes, and on the 28th Riel
repeated his promise that the remainder of the
prisoners captured with Boulton should be released; but suddenly, on the 4th March, swayed
by what motives of policy or revenge it is hard
to say, this capricious tyrant, resolved by one un-
pardonable act to commit his followers beyond
hope of redemption, caused one of the prisoners,
Thomas Scott, to be tried by court-martial. The
mock court, presided over by one Lépine, the
"adjutant-general," condemned him to death, and
with inhuman cruelty his execution was ordered
to take place at noon *the same day*. Deaf to all
entreaties, Riel declared that nothing should save

c

Scott, who, he said, had been unruly whilst in
confinement, and insolent to the "soldiers" and to
him (Riel), and that it was necessary to make
an example in order that Canada should respect
the people of Red River. The execution of the
sentence is thus described in Mr. Donald Smith's
interesting report: "It was now within a few
minutes of one o'clock, and on entering the
Governor's house, the Rev. Mr. Young joined
me and said, 'It is now considerably past
the hour; I trust you have succeeded?' 'No,' I
said, 'for God's sake go back at once to the poor
man, for I fear the worst.' He left immediately,
and a few minutes after he had entered the room
in which the prisoner was confined, some guards
marched in and told Scott his hour was come.
Not until then did the reality of his position flash
upon poor Scott: he said 'Goodbye' to the other
prisoners, was led outside the gate of the fort with
a white handkerchief covering his head; his coffin,
having a piece of white cotton thrown over it,
was carried out; his eyes were bandaged; he continued in prayer, in which he had been engaged
on the way, for a few minutes. He asked Mr.
Young how he should place himself, whether
standing or kneeling, then knelt in the snow, said

farewell, and immediately after fell back pierced by three bullets, which passed through his body. The firing party consisted of six men, all of whom, it is said, were more or less intoxicated. It has been further stated that only three of the muskets were loaded with ball cartridge, and that one man did not discharge his piece. Mr. Young turned aside when the first shots were fired, then went back to the body, and again retired for a moment while a man discharged his revolver at the sufferer, the ball, it is said, entering the eye and passing round the head. The wounded man groaned between the time of receiving the musket-shots and the discharge of the revolver. Mr. Young asked to have the remains for interment in the burying-ground of the Presbyterian Church, but this was not acceded to, and a similar request preferred by the Bishop of Rupert's Land was also refused. He was buried within the walls of the fort. On descending the steps leading from the prison, poor Scott, addressing Mr. Young, said, 'This is a cold-blooded murder,' then engaged in prayer, and was so occupied until he was shot."

After this bloodthirsty display of power, none cared to dispute the authority of Riel, and he ruled the country with a rod of iron.

When the news of this cold-blooded murder
reached Canada, it produced a deep sensation of
horror throughout the length and breadth of the
land. Public meetings were held in Toronto and
other towns in Western Canada, and resolutions
passed urging the Government to despatch an expedition to the Red River to restore the authority
of the Queen and punish the murderers of Scott.
As soon as the delegates from Fort Garry arrived
at Ottawa, two of them, Father Richot and Alfred
Scott, were arrested as accessories before the fact
to the murder of Thomas Scott; but after a formal
examination they were obliged to be released, as
nothing could be proved against them. The
public mind was vehemently excited, more especially in Ontario, to which province Thomas Scott
belonged; and to the previous desire for the acqui-
sition of the fertile prairies of the North-West was
now added in the breast of every patriotic Canadian a deep sympathy with the relatives of the
murdered man, and an ardent longing to avenge
the death of a fellow-countryman, whose only
crime had been loyalty to his Queen and devotion
to his country.

CHAPTER II.

IT having been determined to send a military expedition to restore the authority of the Queen at the Red River, the sanction of the Home Government was obtained for the employment of Imperial troops on this service in conjunction with Canadian militia. An able report had been prepared by the Deputy Quartermaster-General in Canada, Colonel Wolseley, in which he had entered into minute details regarding the composition, equipment, and organization of the force, as well as its victualling, clothing, and transport. In accordance with his suggestions, the expeditionary force, as finally constituted, numbered about 1,200 fighting men, of whom two-thirds were militia, and the remainder regular troops. The latter consisted of the first battalion 60th Royal Rifles, 350 strong ; detachments of Royal Artillery and Royal Engineers, twenty men each, with a battery of four 7-pounder brass mountain guns, and a proportion of the Army Service and Army Hospital corps. The former consisted of two battalions of Rifles, one from each province, raised for two years by voluntary enlistment from the drilled militia. These two battalions were named respectively the 1st or Ontario Rifles, and the 2nd or Quebec Rifles. The regiments of infantry were divided into seven companies of fifty strong (including three officers), with the object of making them more handy and available for boat service by putting each company into a brigade of five boats. The selections for this service were most strict, and none but men of the strongest and hardiest constitutions were permitted to go, it being rightly decided that on an expedition of this nature, about to plunge into an unknown and uninhabited wilderness, every sick man would be a more than ordinary encumbrance.

Early in April 1870, Lieutenant-General the Honourable James Lindsay arrived in Canada as Commander-in-chief, in succession to the late Sir Charles Windham. The selection of this officer was most opportune ; his long previous residence in Canada, and intimate personal acquaintance with the people and the country, rendered him particularly well fitted for the post. Owing to the peculiar "dual" composition of the force, the military arrangements had to be carried out, not by the Imperial authorities only, but also in concert with the Dominion Government, represented in this department by a French Canadian minister, the recognized leader of a party which opposed in every possible manner the departure of the expedition. It therefore required very delicate handling and diplomatic management to make matters work smoothly. A Commander-in-chief new to the country, and unacquainted with its parties and politics, could scarcely have succeeded so well as did General Lindsay.

But he had another and not less important duty to perform, that of selecting the officer to whom the command of the expeditionary force should be entrusted. But here public opinion had been before him. There was an officer in Canada who had already been twice in command of large bodies of Canadian volunteers, and had won the confidence and love of his men, as well as their unhesitating obedience, by his peculiar aptitude for command, and by his happy admixture of the "suaviter in modo" with the "fortiter in re." He was no

novice in the art of war, but had received his
" baptism of fire " in Burmah, and had served in
India, in the Crimea, and in China. The Canadian
volunteers had not forgotten their favourite commander, and the " vox populi " unanimously called
for his appointment as leader of the expedition.
Fortunately, General Lindsay's opinion coincided
with the popular voice, and accordingly Colonel
Wolseley was nominated to the command. Seldom
indeed has any selection met with more general
approval, and assuredly never has it been more
justified by the result.

Early in May, General Lindsay, accompanied
by Colonel Wolseley, repaired to Toronto, where
the force was to rendezvous before its final departure. The enlistment of volunteers for the
Ontario battalion proceeded briskly. The medical
examination of the men was very strict, and
numbers were rejected as physically unable to stand
the fatigues they were expected to undergo. Great
was the disappointment of the rejected, and many a
threatening and angry look was cast on the medical
officers. But so great was the anxiety of the young
men of all classes in Ontario to go to the Red River,
that many, who could not get commissions as
officers, preferred shouldering a rifle in the ranks

to being left behind. Consequently, quite a large percentage of the non-commissioned officers and privates of the Ontario battalion were the equals of their officers in education and social position : notably, of two brothers, one was a captain, the other a sergeant. This equality of social position between officers and men, though in some respects advantageous, yet is not without its drawbacks. It is certainly not conducive to discipline. For instance, I heard a private say to an officer, "Now then, old chap, when you've done with that newspaper just hand it over;" and though no disrespect was intended by the remark, the two probably being old friends or schoolfellows, yet it sounded rather queer.

The Quebec battalion was not so fortunate in its enrolment. The French Canadians, naturally averse to military service, were deterred from enlisting by the exhortations of their clergy, who, in many of the parishes in Lower Canada, publicly dissuaded their flocks from joining a regiment "about to be sent to fight against their brethren in the North-West." They enlisted slowly, and, inasmuch as two-thirds of the officers appointed to the Quebec battalion were French Canadians, the English-speaking Canadians objected to serve under French officers. The ranks filled slowly, and not until enlistment was allowed from Ontario did the battalion complete its numbers, and though nominally a French battalion, yet in reality there were scarcely fifty French in its ranks.

The recruits for the two battalions were sent to Toronto as fast as they were enlisted, and were there formed into companies and served out with arms and clothing, under the superintendence of Colonel Feilden, of the 60th Rifles, to whom their organization had been specially confided.   To his indefatigable exertions and intimate knowledge of the minutiæ of "interior economy," as well as to his kindly demeanour in smoothing over little roughnesses, much of the subsequent good order of these battalions is due.   The grounds of the Crystal Palace, which building had been told off for their accommodation, presented an animated scene, and became the daily rendezvous of the people of Toronto, who were never tired of seeing their citizen soldiery hard at work at drill, and rapidly assuming the appearance and bearing of soldiers.   To their credit be it said, both officers and men took a great interest in their new work, and an honourable spirit of emulation and *esprit de corps* was roused between the two battalions.

Meantime a Land Transport Service was being

organized ; a corps of teamsters was raised, waggons
and carts built, and horses purchased. From the
two batteries of Royal Artillery then under orders
for England, a large number of excellent draught
horses were procured, the remainder being purchased from farmers in the country. Two officers
were specially appointed to the care of this necessary
branch, and the fitting of shoes, harness, and other
details proceeded rapidly.   Each horse was newly
shod and supplied with a spare set of shoes, which
it was hoped would suffice for the fortnight or three
weeks during which they were expected to be in
active work.   Vain hope ! the real state of the road
over which the provisions and *matériel* had to be
carried was known only to the engineer employed
in its construction, and this item of land transport
over a paltry fifty miles was destined to be a source
of the most vexatious delay, even threatening at
one time the success of the whole expedition.

For the actual route from Toronto to Fort Garry
information had been carefully collected from all
quarters. The passage of troops through the United
States territory being of course out of the question,
it became necessary to find a road through British
soil, and the Hudson's Bay Company's officers were
enabled to be of some assistance in this way, as

they were in the habit of proceeding from Canada
to York Factory by a route which passed close to
the mouths of the Red River. The canoe route
usually taken by them was adopted, with one or
two slight changes. By this route the distance is
a little over 1,200 miles; and to accomplish it, it
was necessary that all the means of progression
known to the human race (except that of balloons!)
should be made use of. Conveyance by rail, by
steam-ships, by land transport, and by boats, had
to be provided. The route lay from Toronto by
rail (94 miles) to Collingwood, on the Georgian
Bay; thence by steamer across Lakes Huron and
Superior (534 miles) to Thunder Bay; thence by
land transport over Mr. Dawson's road (50 miles)
to Lake Shebandowan; and from that point in
boats to Fort Garry (550 miles): or, in round
numbers, 1,200 miles.

Of this, the latter portion (600 miles), from
Lake Superior, presented the greatest difficulties,
as the route passed through a wilderness of lakes
and rivers, traversed only by the Indian in his
birch-bark canoe, and never hitherto attempted by
any boat of European construction. Some portion
of this route had been surveyed by Mr. S. J.
Dawson, of the Public Works department, who

was employed in the construction of the road which was to connect the waters of Lake Superior with the innumerable lakes and rivers stretching in an almost unbroken chain to the prairies of the North-West. This gentleman had also published in 1868 an interesting report of this very route, accompanied by maps, with the idea of making it the highway of emigration to the Red River. He was accordingly employed by the Dominion Government in the organization of the "Boat Transport Service," and under his directions upwards of 200 boats were built in the various boat-building establishments in Canada. These boats were of two kinds, "clinkers" and "carvels." They were also of different dimensions, but as a general rule were from 25 to 30 feet long, by 6 to 7 feet wide, and were constructed to carry a weight of 4 tons, besides a crew of 14 men. Mr. Dawson also undertook the onerous task of collecting a body of trained boatmen, skilled in the navigation of boats in rapid water, as it was not of course to be expected that the soldiers should understand this kind of work. He got together about 400 men, who were dignified with the name of "voyageurs," but the great majority of whom were utterly ignorant of their work, and proved afterwards to be only encumbrances in the boats. A very small percentage of them were really "voyageurs," excepting about 100 Iroquois Indians drawn from the villages of St. Regis and Caughnawaga, in the neighbourhood of Montreal, who, with scarcely an exception, were splendid fellows, and without whom it is not too much to say that the troops never could have reached their destination. The boats were fitted with masts and sails, in addition to oars, that they might take advantage of favourable breezes across the lakes, and with arm-chests for the men's rifles and swords; a chest of tools and implements for repairing damages was also provided with each brigade of five boats.[1]

Immediately upon his arrival at Toronto, General Lindsay, accompanied by Colonel Wolseley and the officers of the Control Department, had gone to Collingwood to make the arrangements for the marine transport of the troops from that port across the great lakes to Thunder Bay; and had in one day by dint of hard work inspected the steamers, decided on their different capabilities for the conveyance of troops, and actually concluded a bargain on very favourable terms with their

[1] See Appendix B.

owners, which was telegraphed to Ottawa for the sanction of the Government. Unluckily, that sanction was refused, and the Ottawa Minister undertook the chartering of the vessels himself, with the result of having to pay higher prices than those he had refused to sanction, besides causing a delay of a week or ten days in the hiring of the steamers, and therefore in the starting of the expedition. This little incident will convey an idea of some of the difficulties attending the "dual" organization, that same difficulty which in a greater degree (if Mr. Kinglake is to be believed) attended the earlier operations of the English and French armies in the Crimea, and marred their best-concerted plans.

From Collingwood to Thunder Bay the distance is 534 miles, through Lakes Huron and Superior, and the traffic along this line is carried on by two steamers, the *Algoma* and the *Chicora*, which run every fifth day from Collingwood to Fort William in Thunder Bay. But the waters of Lake Superior flow into Lake Huron through a broad channel called St. Mary's River, which forms the boundary line between British and American territory. This river has very pretty rapids about a mile in length, and to pass these (which are not

navigable for large craft) it is necessary to go
through a canal built on the American side, so
that in fact it is impossible for Canada to get at
her possessions in Lake Superior by water without
passing through American soil.   On the first hint
of difficulties at Red River and the probable
despatch of troops through Lake Superior, the
American authorities at the Sault Ste. Marie not
only refused to allow the troops to pass through
the canal, but even stopped the *Chicora*, on her
regular trip, although she had no contraband of
war on board. This unfriendly attitude caused
much delay and trouble to the expeditionary force,
as it became necessary to land everything on the
Canadian side at the lower end of the rapids,
transport it by land across a three-mile portage,
and re-embark it again at the upper end. For
this purpose the *Algoma*, which, fortunately, had
previously passed the canal, was detained on
Lake Superior at a considerable expense, and an
American steamer called the *Brooklyn* was char-
tered and sent to her assistance.   A glance at the
map will explain the situation, which was most
embarrassing, and necessitated the employment
of two lines of steamers, one on Lake Huron,
the other on Lake Superior, besides the delay

in unloading, transporting, and re-shipping. There can be no doubt that at this time a large section of the American people felt much sympathy for "President" Riel and his "Provisional Government," and were glad of any opportunity to aid him by throwing obstacles in the way of the expedition: hence the closing of the canal; and it was not until the urgent remonstrances of Mr. Thornton had induced the Washington Cabinet to withdraw the obnoxious restriction, that the embargo was removed, and a free passage allowed to all articles not contraband of war. Before this was done, however, several ship-loads of stores had been landed on the Canadian side, and much delay caused thereby.

In consequence of these difficulties Colonel Wolseley despatched two companies of the 1st Ontario Rifles on the 14th of May to form a garrison at the Sault under the command of Lieut.-Col. Bolton, Royal Artillery, the Deputy-Assistant Adjutant-General to the force, for the purpose of superintending the passage of the troops and the transport of the stores across the portage. The departure of these companies, the first detachment of the Red River force which left Toronto, was hailed with delight by the people of Ontario,

D

who had set their hearts on the success of the expedition, and were determined to carry it through. Colonel Bolton arrived safely at the Sault, and immediately set to work to complete the road across the portage and get the stores re-shipped on Lake Superior.

Just at this time the hydra-headed Fenian organization began again to raise its head, and threaten the peace and security of Canada. Two more companies of the 1st Ontario Rifles were therefore sent off on the 16th to increase the garrison at the Sault, and Colonel Bolton was directed to be on the alert to guard against a raid from the American side, as the Fenians had openly declared their intention to annoy and interfere with the expedition. The threatened raid actually took place soon afterwards on the Huntingdon Border, the results of which are well known; and there is no doubt that, had not Colonel Wolseley's foresight and vigilance rendered such an attempt impossible, an effort would have been made to destroy the stores accumulated at the Sault. Had such an attempt been successful, it would have caused such a delay to the expedition as would probably have prevented the return of the regular troops before the winter, if not actually put off the expedition for another year.

The last act of the Canadian Parliament before the recess had been the passing of a bill constituting a portion of the North-West Territory into a new province, under the title of the Province of Manitoba.[1] Amongst other things, this bill provided for the appointment of a Lieutenant-Governor to rule over the new province; and the selection of the man for this office was a subject of much debate and difficulty. The whole of the press of Ontario was in favour of the nomination of a British officer, and pointed out that that officer ought to be the Commander of the expeditionary force, Colonel Wolseley. This view was supported by the Premier, Sir John A. Macdonald; by Sir Stafford Northcote, the President of the Hudson's Bay Company, who was then in Canada; and by Sir Clinton Murdoch, who had been sent out on a diplomatic mission by Lord Granville, and was entrusted with the views of the Home Government on the North-West question. But the French Canadian party were vehemently opposed to such a nomination, desiring that a French Canadian and a Roman Catholic should

[1] See Appendix C.

D 2

be appointed. At this juncture, unfortunately, the Premier fell sick, so dangerously that his life was despaired of: during his illness the whole power of the Cabinet fell into the hands of the French Canadian Minister, Sir George Etienne Cartier. His influence was so great that a compromise between the two parties was effected, and in place of a British officer or a French Canadian, the Honourable Mr. Archibald, of Nova Scotia, was appointed Lieutenant-Governor of Manitoba.

CHAPTER III.

AFTER a stay of seventeen days in Toronto, every
hour of which had been busily spent in the multi-
tudinous details of preparation, matters were at
length in a sufficiently forward state to enable the
first start to be made; and accordingly, on the
morning of the 21st of May, Colonel Wolseley
and staff, and the advanced guard of the expeditionary force, left Toronto for Thunder Bay.
It consisted of Captain Ward's company of the
60th Rifles, and was followed on the afternoon
of the same day by the Head-quarters, and four
companies of the same regiment, under command
of Major Robertson. The embarkation of the
troops took place at Collingwood, the port of
departure, that same evening, on board the steam-
ships *Chicora* and *Frances Smith,* together with

a quantity of stores of all kinds, and about
sixty-four horses with waggons and teamsters for
the Land Transport Service. On board the former
vessel also proceeded Mr. Irvine, the Assistant
Controller in sub-charge of that department, and
Dr. Young, the principal medical officer. The
vessel was crowded with men, horses, boats, and
stores, having on board besides the troops a large
number of voyageurs and workmen for the road
under the charge of Mr. S. J. Dawson, C.E.

The voyage was unmarked by any incident of
peculiar interest, though the scenery was beautiful
and diversified. For some distance the route lay
among islands, now passing through narrow channels
and anon opening out into wide expanses of water,
dotted with innumerable rocky islands of all shapes
and sizes. In the narrowest and prettiest of these
channels the steamer stopped at a little settlement
rejoicing in the romantic name of Killarney.
The deep, narrow channel, the rocky islets covered
with a stunted growth of pines, the pretty little
knot of houses clustering round the village church,
all combined to render the scene highly picturesque
and pleasing to the eye. The charm of novelty,
too, was not wanting: here for the first time we
came across evidences of Indians—a birch-bark

canoe, with two squaws and a "papoose" in it,
and three or four copper-coloured fellows lounging
on the wharf close by. One of the women had fine
regular features of the Circassian type, the other and
the child were certainly ugly, even repulsively so.

The northern portion of Lake Huron is covered
with innumerable islands ; the largest of these,
Great Manitoulin Island, is as large as the Isle of
Wight, with " Jersey, Guernsey, Alderney, and
Sark " (as the school-books say) thrown in. Most
of these islands have no name, and are uninhabited, but at one of them, called " Raspberry
Island," the steamer stopped for a few minutes.
Here an enterprising Yankee had "located" himself
for the cultivation of that delicious fruit, which
grows wild all over Canada, but with more than
ordinary luxuriance on this island. His business
consisted in converting the fruit into jam, which
he exported in enormous quantities to all parts
of Canada and the States, thereby making unto
himself a considerable profit. He came on board
the steamer, and was most affable and amusing,
and invited us to walk up to his house, which
was close by the landing-place, and visit his
establishment. The chief attraction, however,
which he held out to us was a view of his better-

half. "Come up and see my wife," he said ; "I guess she'll astonish you ! Why, sir, she weighs 265 lbs.!" Some of us were not proof against this extraordinary attraction, and paid a visit to the good lady in question, who certainly *did* astonish us ; and, if "raised" on raspberry jam, was a most perfect walking advertisement of the nutritive qualities of that vegetable as manufactured by her enterprising spouse.

A little further on the steamer stopped at the Bruce mines, on the north shore of the lake, and remained there during the night, as the entrance to St. Mary's River is intricate and difficult, the channel winding amongst rocks and islands very pretty to look at by daylight, but unpleasant neighbours on a dark night. Here there is a flourishing village, which has sprung up around the mines in the wonderful mushroom-way in which anything in the way of mining attracts adventurous spirits. The mines are of copper, and said to be very rich and to pay well, notwithstanding the present low price of that metal. Anything more barren, sterile, and unpromising than the country around it would be hard to find, and it is well that bounteous nature has provided riches beneath the surface to compensate for the uncompromising sterility above.

An early start at daybreak on the 23rd soon brought us to the Sault Ste. Marie, commonly called the "*Soo*," as we were informed by the skipper of a steamboat at Collingwood. In course of conversation the name "Sault Ste. Marie" had been frequently mentioned, and a certain restlessness was observable in the said skipper's demeanour at each repetition of the name; at last, however, unable to stand it any longer, and giving his trousers a preliminary hitch, he broke out, "Call it the *Soo*, sir, the Soo! (emphatically): we always calls it the *Soo*; it's ever so much shorter, and everybody will understand ye." And so we called it the *Soo* from that day, not venturing to contend against such unanswerable logic.

The approach to the rapids is very beautiful, but the same marked difference was observable there as everywhere else in America, where the opposite shores of a river or lake belong to different nationalities: on the Canadian side a small and insignificant village, on the American side a thriving town. The explanation of this curious fact, somewhat unpalatable to "Britishers," may be left to wiser heads; but that it *is* a fact, no one will venture to deny. The *Chicora* landed her troops and camp-equipment at the lower end of the rapids on Canadian soil, and then steamed over to the American side to pass through the canal. The "portage" road round the rapids is about three miles long and in good order, much of it having been made since the arrival of Lieutenant-Colonel Bolton. His little force, consisting of four companies of the 1st Ontario Rifles, was encamped about half-way across the portage on a pretty spot of some natural strength. In its front the river, on either flank a deep stream, and in the rear the Hudson's Bay Company's post, abutting on to the main road; so that a surprise by any filibustering party of Yankee-Fenians would not have been so easy to accomplish. On the opposite shore, just across the rapids, half a mile in width, stands the American post of Fort Brady, which is a palisaded enclosure containing a few small guns (not mounted, but used for drill purposes), and garrisoned by 250 men of the 1st United States Infantry (regulars). Previous to the rescinding of the order closing the canal, the American officers had not displayed a kindly feeling, but had done all in their power to obstruct the operations of the expedition. They refused to

allow their own tugs to pass through the canal
if hired by us, and even declined to allow bread
to be baked in their ovens for our soldiers,
although the flour for that purpose would have
been supplied by us. Bread had therefore to be
sent from Collingwood, and the loading of the
steamers at the upper end of the rapids was
much delayed by the want of a tug to tow the
loads to the steamers.

But at the time Colonel Wolseley arrived at the
Sault, an order from Washington had re-opened the
canal to our shipping, and with it had apparently
opened the hearts of our American ·cousins, who
then became most civil and obliging, and willing
to help us in any way. This most desirable change
had been carefully fostered by Lieutenant-Colonel
Bolton and his officers, and consequently the two
garrisons were on terms of cordiality and intimacy,
and quite an *entente cordiale* had sprung up
between them.

Several ship-loads of stores having been landed
at the lower end of the rapids, Colonel Bolton and
his garrison had had their hands full in unloading,
transporting, and re-shipping them. · The men of
the 1st Ontario Rifles had their initiation into
fatigue labour, besides having to furnish guards at

night at both ends of the road and on board the
steamers in the river. Much work had been done
at the upper end of the road by two parties of Mr.
Dawson's men, who were encamped there, and had
built two bridges, a small wharf, and a scow
capable of holding 400 barrels. One of these
parties was composed of Iroquois Indians, engaged
as voyageurs, but employed meantime on any work
of this description. These men worked capitally;
they are plain and simple-minded fellows, obedient
and willing, and splendid axemen, and throughout
the expedition performed yeomen's service.

As the troops re-embarked at the upper end of
the rapids, the scene was full of life and bustle.
The river was full of ships engaged in the work
of transport, and the picturesque beauty of the
scenery was much enhanced by the white tents
and open-air gipsy-looking fires of the camps of
the Iroquois and Canadian voyageurs; whilst, on
the other side of the river, the American town, with
its dark background of forest and hill, threw out
into bolder relief the white and foaming rapids.

The re-embarkation at the upper end did not
take long, and at the same time a company of the
1st Ontario Rifles was put on board the propeller
Shickluna, as a guard for that vessel and the two

schooners she was towing, the *Pandora* and *Orion*, laden with boats and Government stores. About six miles from the Sault the river St. Mary ends, or rather begins, and the broad expanse of Lake Superior stretches out before the eye apparently illimitable as the ocean. The *Chicora* was soon out of sight of land, and pitching and rolling with a fresh north-east breeze and a heavy swell. To all intents and purposes one might as well have been on the ocean; it was difficult to realize that it was only a fresh-water lake, so enormous is its extent :—

" Where their lakes are like oceans in storm or in rest."

The whole of Ireland might be put into Lake Superior (one is sometimes tempted to wish it could be!) and still leave a fair-sized lake.

At daylight on the 25th the high land of Thunder Cape was sighted a long way off, but before reaching it we stopped at Silver Island, a little bit of a rocky islet peeping out of the water like a pin's head. The islet is just large enough for one building over the shaft of the mine, and is said to be a mass of the richest silver ore. It is worked by an American company, who have erected a mill and buildings on the mainland, half a mile

off, and are said to be making a very good thing
out of this little solitary rock. Leaving Silver
Island, we passed close in shore alongside of
Thunder Cape, as the water is very deep. This
promontory rises abruptly to a height of 1,350
feet, and is beautifully wooded to the water's
edge. The approach to the bay is very grand:
on the right, Thunder Cape; on the left, Pie Island
(a curious mountain, 850 feet high, shaped like
an apple pie); and further on, McKay's Mountain,
rearing its massive head to a height of 1,000 feet,
a landmark for many miles to voyageurs descending
the Kaministiquia River. Thunder Bay, of itself an
enormous lake, is but one of the numerous bays
which indent the northern shores of Lake Superior.
It runs in a N.N.E. direction for some twenty or
more miles, and is from twelve to sixteen miles
wide. In these regions everything is on such a
gigantic scale, that the effect of picturesque beauty
is marred. The eye has to travel so far that it
loses the idea of the picturesque in that of the
grand, and can scarcely realize the enormous height
of the hills, owing to the great distance from which
they are beheld. Looking from the western shores
of the bay, the promontory sixteen miles off seems
but like an ordinary hill; it is only when passing

close beneath it, and looking up at it from the deck
of a vessel, that the mind can form an adequate
conception of its vast dimensions, and appreciate
its solemn grandeur. The entrance to Thunder
Bay is guarded by a long island called Ile Royale,
so that the bay is protected from all winds except
those from the south-east. Unfortunately, those
winds appear to be the prevailing ones in summer,
and when blowing fresh produce a heavy surf,
which comes tumbling in in long lines of ugly-
looking rollers, rendering a landing difficult and
somewhat dangerous. There is good anchorage
on a smooth sandy bottom in about three fathoms
of water, and vessels that do not draw more than
ten feet can approach to within 400 yards of the
shore.

Steaming quickly across to the western shores of
the bay, and passing a group of sandy islands
covered with a low scrub, called the Welcome
Islands, we passed on our left the mouth of the
Kaministiquia River, with the clean white buildings
of the Hudson's Bay Company's post of Fort
William shining clearly out against the dark-green
background of foliage, and with the heavy folds
of a huge Union Jack floating lazily in the light
summer air. About four miles further on a small

clearing, with three or four wooden houses and a few tents, marked the beginning of Mr. Dawson's road, the road which was to conduct us to Lake Shebandowan, and so to Fort Garry.

About 10 A.M. on the 25th of May, on a bright and beautiful day, Colonel Wolseley landed on the shores of Thunder Bay, and gave the place the name of " Prince Arthur's Landing," in honour of His Royal Highness, then in Canada. The troops were soon disembarked, a site for the camp selected, and tents pitched; then, stripping to their shirt-sleeves, the men turned to with a will, and horses, oxen, waggons, and stores were quickly landed, the soldiers working heartily till past ten o'clock at night.

CHAPTER IV.

AT PRINCE ARTHUR'S LANDING.

THE first appearance of the country around Prince Arthur's Landing was gloomy and unpromising. A tremendous fire had raged all through this district about ten days previously, devastating the country for hundreds of square miles, and doing much damage to the road. The buildings at Prince Arthur's Landing had been saved from destruction only by the greatest exertions, the fire having burnt as far as the edge of the clearing, which is nowhere more than about 350 yards deep. In place of the green and smiling forest nothing but charred logs and half-burnt trees met the eye, and everything looked black and dismal. But it is an ill wind that blows nobody any good; the fire had destroyed myriads of mosquitoes and black flies, thereby sparing the men much torment and positive pain for some time, until

E

these pests having recovered themselves, returned to their recreation on their human victims.

For the first ten days the weather was delightful, the heat in the daytime being tempered by a cool breeze from the lake; but the nights were cold enough to make one thoroughly enjoy a pipe and a chat round the camp-fire after the labours of the day, and to induce one to pile on the blankets at night.

On the morning after his arrival, Colonel Wolseley, determined to lose no time in making himself master of the situation, started off on horseback to inspect the condition of the all-important road. Mr. Russell, C.E., one of the engineers employed in its construction, accompanied him. They returned at noon on the second day, having ridden as far as the road was then practicable for teams, viz. thirty-one miles. The whole distance to Shebandowan was forty-eight miles, but the road was not intended to be made at first farther than forty-four miles, a footpath only being designed for the last four miles : thus there remained on the 27th of May thirteen miles more of road to be constructed over a hilly and thickly-wooded country, a business involving considerable time and trouble. When at Ottawa, in the month of April, Colonel

PLAN
of
Mr DAWSON'S ROAD
from
Thunder Bay to Lake Shebandown.

Scale, 5 Mile to the Inch.

The figures along the Road shew the
distances from Thunder Bay.

THUNDER BAY

FORT WILLIAM

Seven Mile Creek

Mill Swamp

Little ...

Kaministiquia

River

Kakabeka Falls

Matawin Bridge

St. Brown's Corner

Kemp's Landing

Oskondaga Crossing

Matawin River

Shebandowan L.

Nipigo Landing

Mr McKellar's &c

Wolseley had been positively assured that the road would be open for traffic by the 25th of May, and on this assurance his calculations had been based.

In this forty-four miles the road crosses three large rivers, (as will be seen by the accompanying plan), at distances of twenty-two, twenty-seven, and thirty-nine miles from Lake Superior. For the first twenty-seven miles, as far as the bridge over the river Matawan, the road runs through a partially open country, the woods having been burnt many times along that district. From the appearance of these *brûlés* (burnt clearances), through a succession of which the road passes, it is evident that fires have raged over the country for years past. Some of these *brûlés* are extensive, others only cover a few acres. For the first eighteen miles from Prince Arthur's Landing, the road runs over a succession of sandy hills, with here and there intervening bits of swamp, which, having been well ditched and fascined, are hard and dry, and altogether the best portions of the road. For nine miles further the country is very hilly, of a deep red clay soil, which makes a capital hard road in dry weather, but after rain becomes frightfully sticky and almost impassable. Of so tenacious a nature was this red clay, that it was

E 2

next to impossible to keep the horses properly shod ; and after a journey over the road when in this condition, the horses would return with two or three shoes apiece dragged off by sheer force. The next four miles ridden over by Colonel Wolseley were then being worked at, and would be passable for horses and waggons in a few days. Of the remaining thirteen miles eight only had been cut out through the woods as far as the river Oskondagee (where a bridge of seventy-five feet in length had to be built), and, though just passable for an occasional ox-cart, they were utterly useless for anything like regular traffic. The last five miles had not even been marked out through the woods. The fire of the previous week had done a good deal of damage, having burnt several of the smaller bridges and culverts, most of which however had been partially repaired ; but the most serious damage done was where the road had been cut out along the hill-sides, the made portion having fallen in owing to the crib-work that sustained it having been burnt through. In some places also much of the fascine and corduroy-work had been burnt. Such was the state of the road when the advanced guard of the expeditionary force landed on the shores of Thunder Bay.

On the morning of the 27th, the steamers *Algoma* and *Brooklyn* arrived, and landed the head-quarters and four companies of the 60th They had had a long and disagreeable voyage from Collingwood to the Sault in the steam-ship *Frances Smith*, had lost their way in a fog and got amongst islands, the captain had been drunk the whole time and nearly thrown the ship away, and indeed it was more by good luck than good management that they had escaped shipwreck. On arriving at the Sault, the drunken captain had absolutely refused to go any further without a guarantee of 65,000 dollars, so everything had to be landed there and forwarded by other steamers.

On the afternoon of the same day the *Shick-luna*, with two schooners in tow, cast anchor in the Bay; she brought a company of the 1st Ontario Rifles, which encamped on a little clearing about six hundred yards N.N.E. of the head-quarter camp. A small tug, hired by Mr. Irvine to assist in discharging vessels, also arrived, and the Bay assumed an unwonted appearance of life and bustle. The unloading of the steamers proceeded energetically, horses, oxen, waggons, and stores of all kinds being rapidly landed and removed each to its appointed place. The men of

the 60th worked till 11 P.M. that night with a
hearty goodwill that augured well for the ultimate success of the expedition. The *Algoma* was
unloaded, and enabled to start on the return journey
that night, thereby avoiding detention charges.

The system pursued in unloading vessels was
by means of a large wooden scow, 55 feet long
by 15 feet broad, capable of carrying 500 barrels,
and when loaded drawing only about 18 inches
of water. When calm, vessels could anchor
within 300 yards of the shore, and the scow was
then hauled backwards and forwards from the
vessel to the pier by means of a strong rope.
But when blowing fresh from the east or south-east,
an ugly surf got up in the Bay, which prevented
vessels coming nearer than half a mile or more,
and then the scow was towed backwards and
forwards by the little tug. At the end of the
pier, which was 90 feet long, there was about
three and a half feet of water, so that the scow
could always come alongside the pier, there being
no tide to take into account in these fresh-water
seas. The horses were landed in the same
manner, twenty at each trip, without the slightest
accident of any description. An officer of the
Control Department, Mr. Mellish, had been speci-

ally told off for this work of unloading vessels,
and from being so constantly on board the scow
he acquired the *sobriquet* of the "Admiral."
The heavy old scow had also been christened by
some wag the "Water Lily;" and Admiral
Mellish, and his flag-ship the "Water Lily,"
were well known to every soul in the camp.
Whether from the force of habit or from being
always called the "Admiral," it is hard to say,
but Mr. Mellish would become highly indignant
if any one interfered with him "on board his
own ship." On one occasion, some individual
having presumed to give an order about the
working of the scow, Mellish called out to him
indignantly, "Hold your tongue, sir; do you
command this ship, or do I?" The roar of
laughter elicited by this question awoke him to
the absurdity of the situation, but it was too
late; the joke was too good to be lost, and went
the rounds of the whole camp.

As soon as each scow-load reached the pier, it
was met by strong fatigue-parties of soldiers, who
quickly unloaded the stores, and they were removed
at once in waggons from the wharf, and carefully
stacked in long rows under the hospital marquees
for protection from the weather.

Meantime, strong working parties of soldiers, under the direction of one of Mr. Dawson's staff, were employed in cutting a road to the militia camp, and in a very few days a broad straight road, ditched and fascined, was completed. Another party was employed about half a mile from the camp in altering the main road, which had been originally laid out running straight up a very steep sandy hill. By a slight alteration to the right, the hill was "circumvented" at a much easier gradient. A third party was at work to clear a site near the edge of the lake, for a temporary magazine, clearing the ground of stumps and half-burnt logs, &c. Regularity and method were the order of the day in our miniature Balaclava (unlike its prototype!). Everybody had a certain work to do, and did it. No drones were allowed in the hive.

On the 28th, two companies of the 60th were sent up the road, and were stationed at the bridge over the Kaministiquia River, twenty-two miles off, to work on the bad places of the road. At this bridge there was a very large open clearing, fires having evidently swept over it several times for many years past, and Colonel Wolseley

determined to form here a depôt of supplies, in
consequence of the safety from fire afforded by
the open ground. Stabling for fifty horses was
commenced, and a shed run up for the stores.

On the 31st, the steam-ship *Clematis* arrived,
towing a schooner loaded with 35 tons of hay.
She brought the detachments of Royal Artillery
and Royal Engineers, under Lieutenants Alleyne
and Heneage, a battery of mountain guns, and a
large quantity of ammunition. These guns were
bronze 7-pounders, muzzle-loaders, of the same
pattern as the Abyssinian "steel pens," and as
those recently made for India. They weighed
200 lbs. each, being 50 lbs. more than the steel
guns, but did not require such heavy carriages.
They were made out of the old bronze guns, and
cost only 10*l.* or 15*l.* each, against 44*l.* for the
steel guns. They were parked in front of the
main guard, facing the lake, and soon became the
centre (literally) of an admiring crowd of aborigines
and voyageurs, who, squatting in a circle as near
as the sentry would allow them, seemed never
tired of gazing at these wonderful objects.

The simplicity of the Indians is well illustrated
by a remark made by an old Ojibbeway from the
neighbourhood of Fort William, who happened to

be at the landing-place that day, attracted, no
doubt, by the wonderful stories he had heard
about the Pale-faces. Standing on the pier, in a
dignified attitude, with folded arms, and his
blanket wrapped around him, and showing no
outward sign of astonishment, he watched the
gunners and sappers landing from the *Clematis;*
at last, turning to a friend, he sagely observed,
" What a lot of white people there must be in
the world !"

On the 1st June the remainder of the 60th
arrived in the steamer *Union,* and on the following
day another company of the regiment was sent
up to the Kaministiquia Bridge, making the
third company now stationed there for work on
the road. The first instalment of supplies for the
depôt forming there was sent off in waggons, and
Lieutenant Heneage, Royal Engineers, designed
and commenced a palisaded earth redoubt, 75 feet
long by 45 feet wide, to be built round the magazine as a defensive work for the garrison which
it was intended to leave behind when the force
moved on. Two of the guns were to be mounted
on platforms at the angles of the redoubt,
and the work was designed of such strength as
to enable the garrison to laugh at any Fenian

attempts. Platforms were also made for the transport of the boats; the bodies of the waggons, being taken off the wheels, were joined together by stout pieces of timber, so as to leave the fore and hind wheels some distance apart (much in the way as trunks of trees are carried in England). The boats were hoisted on to the platforms, bottom up, and firmly lashed to the stanchions of the wheels with 2-inch rope, the thwarts resting on cross pieces of wood fixed between the wheels, and the bow of the boat projecting over the back of the horses. The driver sat astride on the keel. This plan was adopted to prevent the boats getting damaged by the severe jolting over the uneven road.

On the 3d June the first four boats were sent off in this way to the bridge over the Matawan River, 27 miles, where they were launched and moored in the river to secure them against fire. This precaution on the part of the commander turned out to be a most happy thought, for just at this time another fire swept over the road between Lake Shebandowan and the Kaministiquia Bridge, destroying the shanties at the Matawan Bridge, and all the hay and stores collected there for Mr. Dawson's workmen. Some of the detached parties along the line even lost their tents, and had to run for their lives. The bridges were saved, but here and there portions of corduroy work were consumed, causing further delay in the completion of the road. The danger from fires thus became a serious element to be taken into calculation.

The head-quarters and four companies of the 1st Ontario Rifles joined the force on the 4th ; with them also came Lieutenant-Colonel McNeill, V.C., the military secretary to the Governor-General, whose services had been placed at the disposal of the General for service with the expedition. A collar-maker also arrived for the Land Transport Corps, whose services were much needed, as many of the horses were suffering from galled shoulders, arising from badly-fitting harness.

About four miles to the south of Prince Arthur's Landing, the river Kaministiquia falls into Lake Superior. On the left bank, and half a mile from the mouth, stands the Hudson's Bay Company's post of "Fort William," of which Mr. McIntyre is the manager. Fort William was an old post of the North-West Company until the amalgamation of that company with the Hudson's Bay, in

1822. It formerly consisted of three or four stone
block houses, surrounded by a wooden palisade
enclosing about fourteen acres of land. The palisade was never required as a protection against
Indians, and gradually fell into decay; but little
of it now remains, and only one block house,
which has been converted into a dairy. The land
is very rich, a good deal of it having been cleared
on both sides of the river. The scenery is pretty;
everything fresh and green, having escaped the
terrible conflagration that had lately devastated
the surrounding country. The river is about 100
yards wide opposite the fort, and is navigable for
ten miles, as far as Point de Meuron. Two miles
above the fort on the right bank is an Indian
mission, a collection of twenty or thirty log huts
inhabited by Indians, who have been converted to
Christianity by the Roman Catholic missionaries,
and half reclaimed from their wild life. They
possess a few cows, and cultivate some patches of
potatoes, but live principally by fishing and trap-
ping, and by voyaging for the Hudson's Bay Company. Some of these Indians are sharp-witted
enough. One of them, called Shab, was quite a
character. Having contrived one day to get hold
of a keg of whisky, strictly contrary to the law

which forbids the sale of spirits to the Indians,
his priest ordered him to give it up, and on
Shab's refusing, reiterated the order, telling him
he must obey the orders of his spiritual pastor;
upon which Shab immediately declared that he had
"turned Protestant," and was no longer under his
authority!   On another occasion he was detected
on Good Friday eating a hearty dinner of meat,
and on being reproached with this infraction
of rules, and told that no "good Catholic"
would do such a thing, Shab replied that he had
a good "Catholic heart" but a "Protestant
stomach!"

About three and a half miles to the north of
Prince Arthur's Landing the Current River falls
into the Bay in a succession of very pretty waterfalls. Three miles from its mouth, but away from
the river, are rich silver mines worked by a company from Montreal. The recent fire committed
sad havoc here, burning down eighteen houses and
some stores of hay. By great exertions the mill
itself, with its new and valuable machinery lately
imported from London, and only erected during
last winter, was saved from destruction. The unfortunate miners lost all they had, many of them
having barely time to save themselves and their

children, so rapid was the advance of the flames. The women and children, to the number of twenty, took refuge in one of the galleries of the mine, where they remained for some time until the fire had passed over.

The northern shores of Lake Superior, though rocky and barren, yet undoubtedly more than compensate for this by the mineral wealth lying hid beneath their surface, awaiting discovery and development by the enterprise of future ages. Copper, iron, lead, and silver have already been found; the last-named metal in great quantities. During the summer of 1870, two metalliferous silver lodes were discovered in the vicinity of Prince Arthur's Landing, for one of which the fortunate owner (who had had the sense to say nothing about it until he had secured the purchase of the land) refused $60,000 (12,000*l.* sterling), expecting to get a much larger sum, which the extraordinary richness of the ore fully warranted.

The commissariat arrangements for the victualling of the troops whilst at Thunder Bay were most satisfactory. Fresh bread and meat and potatoes were issued every day; the bread, which was of a most excellent quality, being baked in field ovens at the camp. Live cattle were brought

from Collingwood and slaughtered daily, that the
men might be spared the salt pork diet as long as
possible. The 60th also opened a canteen, where
good wholesome beer and little luxuries of diet
were procurable, but no spirits. These were from
the first interdicted, with the happiest results.
Officers and men lived on the same rations, and,
with hard open-air work and famous appetites,
sickness was unknown. The daily ration was also
largely supplemented by fish, quantities of which
were caught by trolling with a spoon in the lake
and in the rivers adjoining.

No such thing as a saw-mill existing in the
neighbourhood, sawn lumber (*Anglicè*, planks) for
building purposes had to be brought from Collingwood. As soon as it arrived, stabling for the
horses and sheds for the commissariat stores were
commenced. The rapidity with which Canadian
carpenters run up light buildings of this nature
would astonish a new arrival from "the old country." A couple of days sufficed to put up a stable
large enough for seventy-five horses; and though
the work was not very substantial, yet it answered
the purposes for which it was required well enough.
Storehouses for the immense supplies of pork, flour,
&c., were quickly built, and the former secured

from the danger of being spoilt by the excessive heat of a Canadian summer.

The insufficiency of the Land Transport Corps for the work it had to do had early become apparent to the commander. It consisted of 150 horses and half that number of waggons and teamsters. The horses were, with scarcely an exception, splendid animals; 75 of them had been picked from the Royal Artillery, and the remainder were almost equally good. No transport ever started with a finer lot of animals. But the teamsters had been picked up anywhere and everywhere, without any regard to their qualifications; many of them knew no more about driving or about the care of horses than they did about kangaroos. Some had been bar-keepers, some clerks, and not a few were "decayed gentlemen" who had "seen better days." They were refractory and difficult to manage, being amenable to no discipline. A land transport corps should always, when practicable, be composed of men regularly enlisted and disciplined; only in this way can this most important branch be kept in that state of efficiency so necessary for the movements of an army in the field. For what is the good of an army if the general have not the means of moving it? By

F

careless driving, by ill-fitting harness, and by the
severity of the work, the horses soon began to fall
ill, as many as 35 per cent. being at one time on
the sick list. To relieve the transport had therefore become an object of much solicitude to Colonel
Wolseley, and his attention had been turned to the
possibility of sending boats up by the Kaministiquia River. This had been declared by Mr.
Dawson and others to be a perfect impossibility,
owing to the numerous rapids and falls on that
river; but not content with this opinion, Colonel
Wolseley consulted Mr. McIntyre, the Hudson's
Bay Company's factor at Fort William, who at
once pronounced it to be feasible, though difficult.
Colonel Wolseley immediately decided on trying
the experiment; every boat so sent up represented
another waggon released for the transport of stores;
each waggon could draw from 18 to 20 cwt., and
there were 150 boats to be sent up; consequently
it became a serious element of consideration. Accordingly, at 6.30 A.M. on the 4th of June, thirty-
four men of the 60th, under Captain Young and
Lieutenant Fraser, started to try to get up to Lake
Shebandowan by water. They took with them
four flat-bottomed raftsmen's boats, and two heavy
Quebec-built boats, with thirty-six days' rations.

The tug towed them to Fort William, where Mr.
McIntyre put two Indians into each boat, and gave
them his own guide, a man who knew every stone
and rock in the river from his boyhood.   The
little pioneer force, on the success of which so
much depended, rowed away up the river, bearing the good wishes of all who were sincerely
interested in the success of the Red River
Expedition.

CHAPTER V.

MR. DAWSON'S ROAD.

THE fine weather which had welcomed the
arrival of the expeditionary force, and contributed
so much to render everything jolly and pleasant
in and about the camp, soon disappeared, and
in its place for the next six weeks came heavy
and continuous rain and frequent thunderstorms
of extraordinary severity.

On the 6th June Colonel Wolseley, accompanied
by Assistant-Controller Irvine, made his second
inspection of the road, and penetrated to the
extreme end of it, 37 miles. He returned on.
the 8th, having descended the rapids of the
Kaministiquia River in a canoe, with the object
of judging for himself of the difficulties of the
route and its feasibility as a highway for the
transport of the boats. To his great delight, he

met Captain Young's party just below the bridge, and found that they had successfully surmounted the rapids and falls, and had brought all their boats up without injury. The experiment had turned out a most decided success, so far, and Colonel Wolseley immediately resolved to send the greater part of the boats by this route, and so relieve his transport of a great strain on its resources. Captain Young had cut out all the portages, seven in number, and laid down rollers for dragging the boats over. The portage round the Kakabeka Falls he reported to be a mile in length, for a portion of which distance the boats had to be hauled up a rocky hill, by sheer strength, at an angle of 45°. The labour had been very great, the boats having to be poled and "tracked"[1] up against rapids almost the whole way. The men had been almost constantly wet through— drenched to the skin by rain, and wading up to their waists in the river. They had also suffered severely from flies, for though each man had been served out at Toronto with a small black veil to

[1] "Tracking" is done by means of a long rope fastened to the bow of the boat, which is thus hauled up the rapids by three or four of the crew, who run along the bank where practicable, or wade in the river, the remainder of the crew assisting them at the same time by poling.

shield the face from the attacks of flies, yet
it was found that, for the actual hard work of
tracking and forcing a path along the banks and
through the overhanging bushes, these veils soon
got torn and useless.   But notwithstanding all
these trials and hardships, the men were in excellent health, and as cheery as possible. Captain
Young got his boats up as far as the Matawan
Bridge, beyond which point the Indians declared
that it was impossible to take the heavy boats,
owing to the incessant falls and rapids.

The result of this successful experiment was,
that batches of boats were sent up almost . every
day, or as often as Indians could be got to take
them up, and by the 24th of June 50 boats had
thus been sent up to the Matawan Bridge by
water.

Meantime the work of forwarding the supplies
proceeded steadily though slowly.   A piece of
ground at the Matawan Bridge was cleared,
stabling and sheds hastily run up, and a large
depôt of supplies formed there, as being more
central than the Kaministiquia Bridge.   Every
available waggon was used for this purpose ; no
more boats were sent up by the road, but every
effort was made to collect supplies at the Matawan.

The draught oxen, to the number of 18 span, were sent up from the Bay to the Matawan, and used between that point and the Oskondagee, the road not being passable for horses. A reinforcement of 10 waggons, each complete with a driver and two horses, hired from farmers at Collingwood, was forwarded to Prince Arthur's Landing, at the urgent request of Colonel Wolseley, where they did capital service. The troops were employed on the road, wherever it wanted repair, and companies of the 60th and Militia were encamped all along the line, and worked daily on the road, under the directions of Mr. Dawson and his assistants.

But notwithstanding the energy displayed by the commander, and the hearty way in which he was backed up by officers and men, both regulars and militia, the piles of stores at the Bay instead of diminishing seemed to increase. Each successive steamer brought its load of supplies, which accumulated much faster than they could be sent up.

By the 21st of June, the whole of the troops and stores had arrived at Prince Arthur's Landing; a depôt of supplies was forming at the Matawan, and nearly 70 boats had gone up. But the Matawan was only a little more than half-way to Lake Shebandowan, and the problem was to get the supplies and boats up the other half. A third inspection of the road was made by Lieutenant-Colonel McNeill, on the 15th, and on the 21st Colonel Wolseley rode over it again himself. He found the road between the Matawan and Oskondagee still practically impassable for waggons. A few drawn by bullocks daily passed over it, but no organized horse-transport in the world could have existed, if ordered to work over it regularly with ordinary loads. There were several places that even on horseback were only passed with difficulty. Beyond the Oskondagee, the road was not yet cut to the Dam Site, five miles further, but large gangs of men were at work on it, assisted by two companies of the 60th.

But this failure of the road must not be attributed to want of energy or zeal, on the part of Mr. Dawson, in pushing it forward. The difficulties he had to contend with were many and serious, and his exertions to overcome them and get the road into working order were untiring. Fires twice raged over considerable portions of it, consuming culverts, crib-work, retaining walls, and corduroy-work. Heavy rains swamped it repeatedly, carrying away bridges, and rendering it impassable for days. The road, too, passed over a country where the ordinary facilities for road-making were not procurable; no metalling was attempted upon it anywhere, gravel was only to be found at a very few places, and for miles in some localities even sand was only to be obtained by carting it from a distance. At many places it was necessary to carry the road over swamps and peat-mosses, where deep drains and heavy fascine work were indispensable. It crossed two considerable rivers and numerous large streams, over which bridges had to be constructed. In some districts it passed through a red clay soil of a most tenacious nature, quite impervious to water. After rain, at such places, the first few teams that passed over it cut it up into frightful ruts; and for days afterwards the wear and tear on horses was so great as to stop all traffic. The only portions that stood continuous traffic were those that had been corduroyed; for, although they were rough and only suited for slow draught, still they were passable in all weathers. The grades were tolerably good, as fair as could be expected where all deep cuttings and embankments had been avoided.

Startled by the hopeless nature of the road between the Matawan and Oskondagee, seven or eight miles of which would evidently take a fortnight or more to be in working order, Colonel Wolseley abandoned the idea of sending up stores between those two points, and turned his attention again to the river. The final plan which he adopted was this : at a point called Brown's Corner, five miles beyond the Matawan, he got Mr. Dawson to cut a branch road down to the river, one and a quarter miles, to Calderon's Landing, and put two companies of the 60th on this bit to help the workmen. He organized a naval service under Captain Young of the 60th, who took supplies from the Matawan Bridge in boats, to a point two miles higher up, named Young's Landing : there they were landed and stored under a rude shanty, hastily run up, and were taken on by ox-teams to Calderon's Landing, where they were again embarked, and poled up the river by the 60th to the Oskondagee : from this place they were taken by road five miles further to the Dam Site, where they were again embarked in flat-bottomed boats, and taken up to Lake Shebandowan, four miles further, where they were landed in McNeill's Bay. A path for the

troops was cut through the woods for this last
four miles. All these arrangements, and the little
details connected with them, took some time to
perfect; and it was not until the first week in July
that the branch road to Calderon's Landing, and
the road to the Dam Site, were fit for traffic.

This new system, to which Colonel Wolseley had
been driven as a make-shift, entailed the esta-
blishing of a great number of small posts, at all
of which some kind of rude shelter was necessary
to protect the provisions from the heat. The
frequent change too from boats to waggons, and
vice versâ, could not but occasion some waste and
damage to the barrels by constantly breaking
bulk. The labour gone through by the troops at
this trying period was most excessive; but it
was done in such a cheerful, soldier-like way as
to extort the admiration of everyone. Colonel
Wolseley himself thus writes of the 60th at this
time: "The men and officers have worked in a
way that I have never seen soldiers do before;
they are all as cheery as possible, and seem to
enjoy the life, which is assuredly no easy work."
And again: "I have just heard from McNeill,
who is encamped at the Dam Site; he is loud
in his praises of the 60th, as indeed everyone

must be, who has seen them work here!" The militia, too, vied with their brethren of the regulars, and one and all nobly followed the example set them.

Although the proceedings of the little expedition, which was forcing its way by sheer hard work against all obstacles far away in the depths of the North American wilderness, had attracted but little notice in England, yet amongst military men it was an object of some attention, and a great desire had been manifested to join the expedition amongst some of the more restless spirits in our army, some of that class of men who have not yet, thank God! been driven out of our ranks by the efforts of would-be Army reformers. An officer of the —th Lancers, Captain M——, being unable to get regular employment with the force, resolved to join it as a volunteer; and, getting a few months' leave of absence, actually crossed the Atlantic, and made his way to Prince Arthur's Landing, anxious to see a little service in these piping times of peace. Though contrary to the orders on the subject, Colonel Wolseley had not the heart to refuse his request after such a long journey, and allowed him to accompany one of the brigades of boats

as a volunteer, giving him charge of a boat's crew.
It was on a pouring wet morning that the brigade
of boats which he accompanied started from
Prince Arthur's Landing to work their way up
the Kaministiquia River : drenched to the skin,
presenting a most dejected and forlorn appearance,
but full of pluck and resolution to carry out
his purpose, the little Lancer stepped into his
boat in happy ignorance of what was before him.
The next thing that was heard of him was from
Colonel Wolseley, who met him at the Kakabeka
Falls, still wet through, but manfully hauling away
at a rope, and dragging his boat up a hill 120
feet high and as steep as the roof of a house.
He had been six or seven days getting that distance, and had scarcely had a dry stitch on him the
whole time ; he afterwards confided to me, that
at that time he had had quite enough of the
Red River Expedition, and fully expected the
Colonel would have offered him a seat in his
canoe back to Prince Arthur's Landing, an offer
which he would have jumped at ; but, as he did
not, he had to go on, and finally reached the
Matawan Bridge after a tremendous journey of
eleven days. We were encamped at the Matawan
when he appeared there, and hailed his arrival

with much pleasure and friendly chaff. One friend hoped he had "enjoyed his pic-nic;" another suggested the advisability of a visit to his tailor; a third hoped he had not caught cold; &c. &c. The rapids of the Kaministiquia had certainly wrought a magical change in the spruce and neat appearance of our little Lancer Volunteer. His garments had a most dilapidated appearance, out at knees and elbows, and would scarcely have commanded an excess of gratitude if bestowed on the veriest tramp in England. But he was jolly and hearty, and declared he had never been better in his life, and on the whole rather *liked* being wet through. We were rather amused at a story told of him during this "pleasure trip." He was lying awake in his tent one night, so bothered by the mosquitoes as to be unable to sleep, tired as he was. At last he got up and seized what he took to be the bottle of mosquito oil, and smeared his hands, neck, and face with its contents. Next day at dinner-time, one of the party, when about to help himself to the Harvey Sauce (a great luxury, and carefully husbanded for the sake of the salt pork), cried out, " Hullo! some one's spilt a lot of the Harvey Sauce!" On careful inquiry, poor M—— turned out to be the delinquent.

It was Harvey Sauce, and not mosquito oil, with which he had anointed himself the night before! But, notwithstanding these little troubles, he subsequently followed the expedition to Fort Garry, and worked his way there like the rest of us, though as a pleasure trip some might think it a curious way of spending four months' leave.

Whilst on this subject of getting wet, I may mention that, though all had to go through it, *nolens volens,* yet there was one officer of the 60th, F——, who positively appeared to delight in it, and was never thoroughly happy unless he *was* wet through. He used to wear a pair of untanned seal-skin mocassins, which, being waterproof, would have thereby seriously interfered with his pleasure : to obviate this inconvenience, and I suppose not to give his feet an unfair advantage over the rest of his body, he used to fill these mocassins full of water every night, and place them outside his tent, where they mounted sentry like a pair of "tops" on their trees. Of course the leather got thoroughly soaked with water, and his feet could not by any possibility ever be dry. He was employed with Captain Young on the boat service, where he worked like a horse from morning to night; and being always in and out of the water, tracking up rapids and so forth, he was quite "in his element," and intensely and thoroughly happy. He never appeared to be the worse for this amphibious mode of life, and rheumatism had as yet no terrors for him.

To the north and west of Lake Superior, the country rises gradually to a height of from 800 to 1,100 feet above the level of the lake. This rugged Laurentian country is called the Height of Land, and forms the great watershed of the northern portion of the Continent. Here the waters of the Ottawa, and the northern tributaries of the great lakes, interlace with those flowing into Hudson's Bay. The change is most marked; once over the dividing line, and every stream and river flows to the west and north instead of to the east. Lake Shebandowan itself is 800 feet above Lake Superior. It may therefore easily be imagined that rivers flowing from this height into Lake Superior, only fifty miles off, must be very rapid. Up this height the boats had to be dragged, and the stores conveyed; some idea may therefore be gained of the labour involved. The yearly rainfall in this section is very great—frightfully great, if the time we spent in this region be any criterion; for, during the month of June,

and up to the 16th of July, when the first brigade
of boats left Shebandowan, it rained on fifteen
days in June, and on eight out of the sixteen in
July. Thunder-storms of extraordinary severity
swept over Thunder Bay, recurring on an average
about every other day with unpleasant regularity,
and accompanied by rain such as is seldom seen
out of the tropics. Rightly indeed has it been
named "Thunder Bay!" It would rain sometimes
for two or three days together in such a manner
as to stop all traffic on the road. The Kaministiquia River rose six feet in one night, several
bridges were swept away, and much damage done
to the road. About this time affairs looked rather
dismal, and the chance of ever getting away in
the boats seemed more and more distant. Even
the most sanguine began to feel gloomy fore-
bodings, for the summer was rapidly passing, and
Fort Garry seemed as far off as ever. There
were not wanting, too, a few croakers, who declared
that the idea of a return from Red River this
year was absurd, and that the expedition would
never reach its destination before the winter frosts
set in. But throughout all, the commander was
sanguine of ultimate success; and to every
question of when the start would be made,

replied invariably, "As soon as I have a hundred and fifty boats, and two months' provisions at the Lake."

Amongst the many little details of arrangement which had to be provided before leaving Toronto, Colonel Wolseley had had made, and issued to each man of the expeditionary force, a small black veil to protect the face and neck against the bites of flies. These veils were made of very fine black netting, and when put on were kept tight round the head and throat by a bit of elastic; a piece of hoop sewn in the centre kept them off from the face. For ordinary bush-work they answered very well, but soon got torn by the rough work of tracking. A quantity of mosquito-oil for anointing the hands, neck, and face, was also provided, and a large canful put into each boat.

These precautions had been taken in consequence of the dreadful tales told about the flies in the Lake Superior region. These flies were of four kinds, mosquitoes, black flies, sand-flies, and deer-flies. The mosquito is so well known throughout almost the whole world (with the exception of our own favoured isle) that it needs no description. The black fly is a small insect, like a very small house-fly, and abounds in

the Canadian woods, where it is a terrible
torment. It chiefly attacks the back of the neck,
and throat, wrists, hands, &c., but is not particularly fastidious. It draws blood at every bite,
and the part bitten swells up and becomes very
painful. The black fly, however, bad as he is,
is decidedly preferable to the mosquito, for he
is a gentleman and goes to bed at night, whereas
the mosquito bullies the unhappy victim even
more at night than in the daytime. Dead tired,
and thoroughly worn out by a long day's rowing,
poling, and tracking, in some localities one was
so bullied by these intolerable pests as to be kept
awake all night; and in place of a sound and
refreshing sleep, one would get up in the morning
bitten all over, and feverish and cross. On one
occasion, I had to ride to the Kaministiquia
Bridge with an order, and on arriving there at
9.30 P.M., found the few men who had not turned
in sitting round the camp-fire with their veils
on, as if they were going to take a hive of bees.
I was rather inclined to laugh at these precautions,
for at Prince Arthur's Landing we were not
troubled with flies, but I soon found out my
mistake: very little sleep did I get that night;
the mosquitoes held high jubilee over me, and

never did I feel more inclined to cry out with
the Psalmist, "Would God it were morning!"
At the first streak of daylight I crawled out from
my wretched lair, and plunged into the river to
relieve my heated and feverish frame. Those who
have not experienced the mosquito in his native
fastnesses, can have no idea, no conception of an
idea, what an intolerable nuisance he can make
himself. I was once enjoying an evening's fishing
on a charming little trout stream; the trout were
biting freely, but so were the mosquitoes, which
swarmed around me in myriads, fastening eagerly
on wrists, hands, and face. Tempted by the
sport, I continued fishing, until my eyelids were
so swollen that I could scarcely see out of my
eyes; at last, in despair, I fairly made a bolt of
it, and ran away without waiting to put up my
rod, regularly put to flight by the mosquitoes.
The third species of plague we had to contend
against were sand-flies. These minute insects, so
small as to be scarcely perceptible, are great
torments : no veil or netting will keep them out;
they are so small that they can crawl through anything. Their bite is as if you had been rubbed
over with cayenne pepper; you feel a sudden
burning, and have some difficulty in discovering

the enemy, so diminutive is he. The French Canadians very aptly call them *brûlot*. The deer-fly is a large mustard-coloured insect, three-quarters of an inch long, and furnished with nippers. He takes a piece of flesh right out when he bites, and will fight you like a wasp or a bee. Horses become perfectly mad from their bites. Towards nightfall the mosquitoes and sand-flies are especially attentive, and the only way to escape them is to make a big smoke,—"faire un boucane," as the French say,—and sit in it; a remedy scarcely less disagreeable than the disease. We used to smoke our tents out regularly before turning in at night, and if you did not do so, woe to your hopes of sleep!

On the 29th June, the Lieutenant-General arrived at Prince Arthur's Landing, on a visit of inspection; and, accompanied by Colonel Wolseley, rode over the whole road as far as the Dam Site, and went up to Lake Shebandowan in a canoe. He returned by the river Kaministiquia, running the rapids in a canoe. In his passage down the river the Lieutenant-General passed four brigades of boats, at different places, working their way up against the rapids. The labour at this time was exceptionally severe, owing to the excess of water

in the river, which had become so deep that it
was difficult to pole; and, as the banks were
flooded, tracking was extremely difficult and
laborious.   The former tracking path, cut by
previous boats' crews, was three feet under water.
One of these brigades, having camped one evening
on an island, was compelled by the rising of the
river to take to their boats in the middle of the
night, and cross to the mainland; next morning
the island was not to be seen! In its place was
a foaming rapid. For four days no waggon train
of supplies could be sent up the road. The
Lieutenant-General left again on the 4th of July,
by steamer. His visit was of great benefit to
everyone, and as he arrived in the midst of a
very severe storm, he was fully enabled to judge
of the difficulties which the men of the expedition were contending against, on the road and on
the river.

At the time that the Lieutenant-General arrived
at the Matawan, on his visit of inspection, I
happened to be present, and was much amused
at the dress in which the inspecting officer was
received, by Captain Young, who was then at his
daily work in the boats taking supplies up the
river. His dress consisted of but three articles:

a red woollen night-cap; a flannel shirt, open at
the throat and chest, with the sleeves rolled up
to the elbows; a pair of duck trousers tucked
up to the knees, and confined round the waist
by a leathern belt and sheath knife; no shoes or
stockings, and a pipe in his mouth, which he
politely removed to shake hands with the General!
At this time the Matawan River had overflowed
its banks; the water was a foot deep right under
the rude table on which the officers ate their
daily rations of salt pork and biscuits; in fact,
it was a matter of some difficulty to keep your
feet out of the water. But this, too, had its advantages, when looked at from the "Mark Tapley"
point of view; for, when you were thirsty, you
had nothing to do but dip your tin cup under
the table and bring up a cupful of water.
F—— used to enjoy it very much, as he never
made any attempt to keep his feet out of the
water, and was able to be in his normal state of
wet without extra trouble.

One more anecdote about "Jack Young."
Though always the first man to jump out of a
boat in a rapid, utterly regardless of the depth
of the water, and generally wet to the waist, yet
he had the old soldier's knack of keeping his

pipe and matches dry, and was always ready
with a light for anybody's pipe. One day he had
been up to his chin in the river, and on getting
into the boat again, was asked by one of the men
(who thought to take a "rise" out of him) for a
light for his pipe. He immediately pulled off his
woollen night-cap, in the loose end of which he
had stowed his pipe and tobacco and matches, and
gave the man a light for his pipe! Is it a matter
of wonder that the men, who always take their
cue from the officers, worked as they did, with
hearty good-will and good humour?

Mr. Donald Smith, who had succeeded the late
Mr. McTavish as Governor of the Hudson's Bay
Company, had arrived at Fort William on his
way to "Norway House," and to him Colonel
Wolseley entrusted the delivery of a proclamation,
which he had drawn up, to the Red River people.
Mr. Donald Smith undertook to send it into the
settlement, by a safe hand, from Fort Alexander,
at the entrance to Lake Winnipeg. The proclamation was as follows :—

To the Loyal Inhabitants of Manitoba.

Her Majesty's Government having determined upon stationing
some troops amongst you, I have been entrusted by the Lieutenant-
General commanding in British North America, to proceed to Fort
Garry with the troops under my command.

Our mission is one of peace, and the sole object of the Expedition is to secure her Majesty's sovereign authority.

Courts of Law, such as are common to every portion of her Majesty's Empire, will be duly established, and justice will be impartially administered to all races and all classes; the loyal Indians and Half-breeds being as dear to our Queen as any other of her loyal subjects.

The force which I have the honour of commanding will enter your Province representing no party either in religion or politics, and will afford equal protection to the lives and property of all races and all creeds.

The strictest order and discipline will be maintained, and private property will be carefully protected.

All supplies furnished by the inhabitants to the troops will be duly paid for.

Should any one consider himself injured by any individual attached to the force, his grievance shall be promptly inquired into.

All loyal people are earnestly invited to aid me in carrying out the above-mentioned objects.

(Signed)   G. J. WOLSELEY, *Colonel,*

Commanding Red River Expeditionary Force.

PRINCE ARTHUR'S' LANDING, THUNDER BAY,
    June 30th, 1870.

Copies of this proclamation were sent to the Protestant and Roman Catholic Bishops at Red River, and to the Hudson's Bay Company's officer at Fort Garry; and, at the same time, Colonel Wolseley urgently besought these gentlemen to endeavour to open up a cart-road from Fort Garry to the north-west corner of the "Lake of the Woods," a distance of about ninety miles. At the request of Colonel Wolseley, Mr. Dawson wrote at the same time, urging the immediate commencement of this work, and promising that the Public Works' Department would defray the expenses of such road. Little or nothing, however, was done, and the troops eventually had to descend the dangerous rapids of the Winnipeg River, and make a long circuitous voyage round the southern shores of Lake Winnipeg, and up the Red River.

The serious number of horses rendered unfit for work through collar-galls, had induced Colonel Wolseley to request that twenty sets of straps, for converting double-collar harness into breast-draught harness, should be sent him. Through some misunderstanding at Montreal, in the absence of the Lieutenant-General, only seven breast-straps were sent, and these were of the kind used in field batteries, for the non-commissioned officers' horses, only intended to assist gun teams for a short distance over difficult ground, and quite un-fitted for heavy and continuous draught. Had the twenty sets applied for been sent, it would have enabled our transport to make use of forty horses daily more than they were then doing, for we had constantly that number of horses on the sick list, incapacitated for work owing to galled shoulders, but otherwise in good working con-dition.

In organizing a horse-transport service, this subject is well worthy of attention; at least 20 per cent. of the harness provided should be fitted for breast-draught, so that the moment a horse shows signs of a collar-gall, the collar may be replaced by the breast-straps, and *vice versâ*. By these means, if due care be taken, no horse need ever be on the sick list from galled shoulders.

On the 5th July, Colonel Wolseley moved his head-quarters to the Matawan Bridge, and on the 13th advanced to the Dam Site or "Ward's Landing," 17½ miles further, and three miles from Shebandowan Lake. At this late period, the so-called "road" between Brown's Corner and the Oskondagee, a distance of seven miles, was still very bad. In many places it was almost impassable, nothing but a track through the woods, unditched, uncorduroyed, and with stumps of trees and boulders of rock still in the centre of the "road." The wisdom of Colonel Wolseley's resolution to abandon the use of this part of the road as a means of transporting his supplies, and to devote all his energies to the utilization of the river, was thus amply proved. Had he waited for this part of the road to be in working order, the expedition would have been still further delayed, and might have been still struggling through the portages and rapids of the Winnipeg; in any case, the regular troops could not have returned this summer, but must have wintered at Fort Garry.

About this time (5th to 10th July) the whole of the force was scattered about all along the line, both on water and on land. Some were working on the road, encamped by companies, wherever repairs were required; some were taking boats up the river to the Matawan Bridge, some were taking stores from the Matawan to Young's Landing, and others from Calderon's Landing to Ward's Landing. To feed these numerous detached parties all along the road was no easy matter, and took up a great deal of the available transport; but Mr. Irvine's arrangements were so good, and he was so well backed up by Captain Nagle and those under him, that there was never any complaint made of want of rations. Field bakeries were established at Prince Arthur's Landing, at the Matawan, and at Ward's Landing; and the bread baked by the men of the Army Service Corps was most excellent.[1] Colonel Wolseley writes on the 16th July: " I have never

---

[1] The Field oven put up at Ward's Landing turned out in twelve hours 470 rations of bread, in 1½ lb. loaves.

before been with any force in the field so well fed
as this one has been up to the present time.
The rations are good and ample ; the absence of
any spirituous liquor, as part of the daily issue,
is marked by the excellent health and spirits of
the men ; and, I may add, by a remarkable absence
of crime!" Great praise indeed, coming from
one so well qualified to judge!

CHAPTER VI.

ALTHOUGH the failure of the road had occasioned much delay, through the necessity of conveying the boats by water, yet as there is seldom any evil in this world without its attendant good, so it had been of much service to the troops, in accustoming them to the boats, and breaking them in to the severe labour of poling and tracking. It had also been the means of opening the eyes of the officers to the deficiencies of the voyageurs. As has already been mentioned in a former chapter, these men were a motley crew, collected from all parts of Canada, without much regard to their qualifications as boatmen. The Iroquois Indians, and some of the Lower Canadians from Three Rivers, were about the only good boatmen out of the lot, and, as rations had to be carried in the boats for every man who embarked at Shebandowan, so it became an object of some importance that none but skilled voyageurs should be taken. The most stringent orders on this head had been issued by Colonel Wolseley, and officers commanding brigades were directed to leave at the first portage they came to, all *soi-disant* voyageurs whom they found to be incapable of managing boats. The object of having voyageurs was not to pull an oar, a duty which the soldiers were quite competent to perform, but to take the management of the boats in rapid water, and to instruct the soldiers. Many men had engaged themselves under the high-sounding title of voyageurs, with the object of working their passage to Red River by their manual labour at the oar; consequently, when they had to take hold of a paddle or a pole, they were found to be quite ignorant of its use. Numbers of them were therefore rejected, and not allowed to embark in the boats, greatly to their disgust.

The Indian voyageurs, the Iroquois, were well worthy of the name, and were employed for a long time in taking up boats and stores from Ward's Landing to McNeill's Bay, a distance of three miles, but a very hard bit of water, there being no less than six rapids in that short distance. Their

"boss," old Ignace, was a fine old fellow, one of
Nature's noblemen; most dignified, quiet, and gentlemanly, and a splendid man to steer a boat down
a rapid. He had been one of Sir George Simpson's
men, and had also accompanied Dr. Rae in his
Arctic explorations. He had grey eyes, a very rare
feature in an Indian. His men obeyed him readily,
and when any little thing was wanted from them,
a word from Ignace was sufficient. They required,
however, careful treatment, as they were quite
aware of their own importance to the expedition,
and though inclined to work hard, yet not unnaturally objected to extra hours. Every day being of
importance, they were ordered to continue their
work on Sundays, which at first they flatly refused
to do. Their objections were got over by the promise of an extra day's pay for the extra day's
work; and thus was the Indian tempted by
his white brother to violate the convictions
of his conscience. By dint of energy and hard
work, boats and provisions were forwarded
rapidly to McNeill's Bay, as fast as they arrived
from the Oskondagee: each boat, before it was
sent up, being thoroughly overhauled by the
boat-carpenters, and the damages sustained in
the passage up the rapids carefully repaired.

The 16th July had been the day fixed by Colonel
Wolseley some time before, for the first start to be
made from Lake Shebandowan, but as the day
approached it became very doubtful whether such
was possible. Lieutenant-Colonel McNeill had been
for some time at the lake, and had pitched his
camp on the shores of a pretty little bay with a
charming sandy beach, which had been named
after him, "McNeill's Bay." Here he had been in-
cessantly at work, assisted by Mr. Myer and Mr.
Jolly of the Control Department, getting things
into order; and as far as the military arrangements were concerned, everything was ready for
the despatch of the first three brigades. But
much confusion reigned in the civilian department—boats, voyageurs, boat-gear, and guides.
Poor Mr. Dawson worked untiringly, and did all
that one man could do to carry out Colonel Wolseley's wishes, but he had a weak and inefficient
staff of assistants, only one of whom, Mr. Graham,
appeared to be of any use. The boats kept arriving in batches at McNeill's Bay, and Mr. Graham
had to overhaul them and fit each one with its
complement of masts, sails, rowlocks, oars, and
other gear. There was great confusion in this department, many of the things not having been sent

H

up from Prince Arthur's Landing, and the boat-sails having been used for the last two months as tents for the numerous working-parties all along the road; the result was that the soldiers had to do all the work themselves, and worked hard all day on the 16th cutting masts, bending sails, and fitting oars to rowlocks, &c. The scene at McNeill's Bay was full of bustle and excitement; boats were loading at the little wharf, others drawn up on the beach to be fitted with masts and sails, others that were loaded and ready were moored at a little distance from the shore. Tents were being struck and packed, and the last preparations made for the long-looked-for embarkation. About five o'clock in the evening Colonel Wolseley himself went up to the lake to superintend the final departure. At that hour it appeared quite hopeless to get the brigades off that day, but Colonel Wolseley reiterated his orders, and declared that the boats *must* start, if they had to go on working till midnight. By degrees each boat got on board its complement of stores,[1] and dropped out and moored in the bay to make way for the next one, but it was half-past eight o'clock in the evening before they were all ready to

[1] See Appendix D for a list of stores embarked in each Brigade at Lake Shebandowan.

start. There were three brigades of boats, A, B, and C, seventeen in all, containing two companies of the 60th, under Captains Young and Ward, and the Royal Artillery and Royal Engineers, under Lieutenants Alleyne and Heneage, the whole being under the command of Colonel Feilden of the 60th. Each boat had two voyageurs in it, besides eight or nine officers and soldiers, and carried sixty days' provisions for all its crew. The men were delighted at the prospect of getting away, and cheery were the farewells to less fortunate comrades left behind. "Good-bye, Jim. No more poling now for some time." "Hurrah for Fort Garry!" and the silent woods rung for the first time to the echoes of a British cheer.

It was an evening of surpassing loveliness; the wind, which had been blowing fresh all day from the west, had gone down, and the lake lay calm and smooth as a mirror, reflecting in its placid bosom the varied tints of a mellow sunset, which tinged the fleecy clouds with wondrous hues. The measured dip of the oars, and the last faint hurrahs of the boats' crews, alone broke the calm glory of the summer evening, as we stood on the little wharf and strained our eyes to catch the last glimpse of the fast disappearing boats, the vanguard

H 2

and pioneers of the Red River Expeditionary Force. "Thank God! they are off at last." Deep and fervent were the ejaculations of thankfulness expressed by every one, but to none did the sense of relief come home so directly as to the heart of the Commander, who, having borne the burden and heat of the day during the last trying weeks of suspense and anxiety, at length began to see the fruition of his hopes, and the reward of his unremitting toil and anxious care.

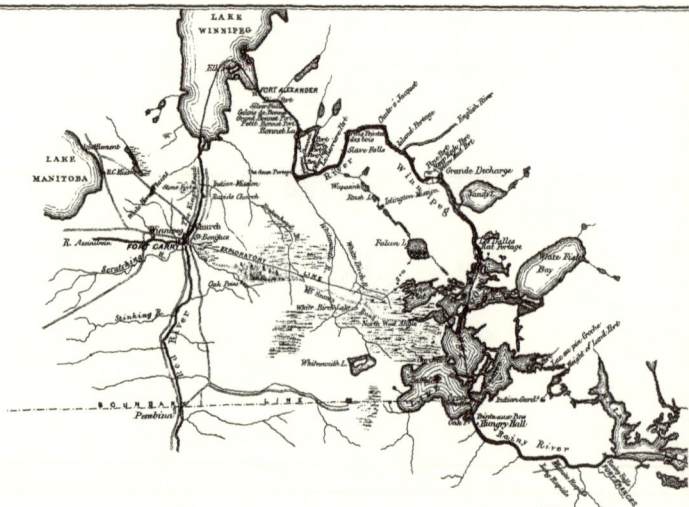

Plan of
Route followed by
RED RIVER EXPEDITIONARY FORCE
FROM
LAKE SUPERIOR TO FORT GARRY,
during the summer of 1870.

CHAPTER VII.

EN VOYAGE.

"Arma virumque cano."
"Arms, men, and canoes."—*Free Translation.*

AT last the ice was fairly broken. The departure of the first three brigades on the 16th of July was followed by two more, D and E, on the 17th, F on the 18th, G on the 19th, and so on. The whole force was divided into twenty-one brigades, which were distinguished by the letters A, B, C, &c., each brigade being composed of six boats.[1] The companies of the 60th followed each other in quick succession, then the 1st Ontario Rifles, and lastly the 2nd Quebec Rifles. Lieutenant-Colonel McNeill, V.C., remained at Shebandowan, superintending the embarkation until the whole of the brigades had left, when he and Mr. Jolly of the Control Department followed in a light

[1] See Appendix E.

bark canoe. By the 1st of August the last brigade, X, had embarked. On this day the leading brigades had reached Bare Portage, 150 miles from McNeill's Bay, the other brigades being scattered along the intermediate distance. Colonel Wolseley himself remained until he had seen the whole of the regulars and the first two brigades of militia embark, and then started himself on the 23rd of July, accompanied by Mr. Irvine, in a birch-bark canoe, manned by Iroquois Indians, to catch up Colonel Feilden and the leading detachment.

The route followed by the force (as will be seen by the accompanying sketch) differed slightly at the commencement from the old canoe route of the Hudson's Bay Company. The new route, first discovered by Mr. S. J. Dawson, passed through Lakes Shebandowan and Kashaboiwe, crossed the Height of Land by one of the lowest passes, and turning westward into Lac des Mille Lacs there joined the old canoe route, which it followed for the remainder of the way to Red River.

To attempt to describe for the benefit of the general reader the scenery and incidents of the route, it is necessary to relate what I myself actually saw and did, at the risk of the too frequent repetition of the word " I." Accordingly, at half-past six

on the evening of the 21st July, I left McNeill's Bay
in Colonel Wolseley's gig, accompanied by Lieutenant Denison of the Canadian Militia and a crew
of six men, four of whom belonged to the 60th, the
other two being voyageurs, one of them an old
Iroquois Indian.   We had no guide, for Mr. Dawson
had failed to procure any from Fort William, but in
lieu of a guide we had a rough tracing on paper of
the configuration of the first two lakes and portages
as far as Lac des Mille Lacs.   It was a lovely
evening, and as we pulled quietly along and set our
little lug-sail to a favouring breeze, the novelty of
the situation as well as the picturesqueness of the
scenery were most inviting.   Here we were, eight
persons in a small gig (a very jolly little craft about
thirty feet long and pulling six oars), with thirty
days' provisions, bound for Fort Garry, 600 miles
off.   None of us had ever been there before, and
our only guide was a map and a compass.   Lake
Shebandowan is about twenty miles long, a large,
long lake, or rather three long lakes joined together
by narrow channels.   We were told to hug the
north shore, which we did until nightfall, when we
landed at the first likely spot and bivouacked for
the night.   The north shore of the lake has been
repeatedly swept by fires at various intervals for

many years past; and the blackened and branchless trunks of trees left standing here and there, sometimes in great numbers, present a strange weird appearance, like ghostly witnesses of a bygone vegetation. On the south shore the woods have been little injured by fire, but their growth is small, bespeaking a poverty of soil, which is fully borne out by the patches of bare rock cropping out here and there, covered with a scanty growth of moss. Wild raspberries are abundant, flourishing best on the burnt districts. All these Canadian lakes are very much like one another, and when covered with islands and indented with deep bays it is most difficult to find one's way about them. We lost our way twice on Lake Shebandowan, but fortunately soon recovered the right track, and reached the east end of the portage road which leads into Kashaboiwe Lake, about 10 A.M. on the 22nd.

Here we found three brigades, one occupied in portaging[1] its boats and material, and the other two waiting for their turn to do the same. The stoppage

[1] As the word "portage" will be found frequently recurring in these pages, it would be as well to explain that it means a break in the navigation between two lakes or rivers, and that boats, provisions, &c. &c., have to be "portaged" or *carried* over this break. There were no less than forty-seven "portages" between Lake Shebandowan and Fort Garry, each one entailing very severe labour on the troops.

originally arose in front, from the fact of the first
detachment being unavoidably large, and from the
Royal Artillery having, in addition to their provisions, two 7-pounder guns, and a quantity of
ammunition and military equipment, which occupied much time in portaging. The brigades also
were at first sent off rather too quickly one after
the other from McNeill's Bay, so that those in front
had not time to get over the portage before the
next detachment arrived.

The Kashaboiwe Portage is about 1,500 yards
long. When we arrived we found that a broad
road had been cut through the woods, and
skids or rollers laid down on which to haul
over the heavy boats. This work had been
done by Colonel Feilden's detachment, which
led the way all through, and had the honour
of pioneering the force and cutting out all the
portage roads.

The labour of portaging was very severe; everything had to be carried across on the backs of the
men. For this purpose, Indians and experienced
voyageurs use a long strap called a "portage strap,"
which consists of a broad thick band of ox-hide
leather, 26 inches long and 3¼ inches broad, taper-
ing off at both ends to one inch in breadth. To

each of these ends is sewn a long leather strap about one inch wide and five to seven feet long, the whole forming one long strap. It is used thus. The long ends are tied firmly round the barrel or package to be carried, in such a manner as to leave at the broad part of the strap a loop large enough to allow the head to be passed through. The barrel is then hoisted on to the back, and the broad part of the strap rests against the forehead. In this way almost the whole strain bears on the backbone and vertebræ of the neck. An Indian usually clasps his hands round the back of his head to help the " leverage," and in this manner will carry an immense weight. Our men at first were rather awkward at it, and could not carry a great weight, but they got into the way of it very quickly, and before they got to Fort Garry would think nothing of a weight which at first they would have been physically unable to stagger under. Our barrels, or rather half-barrels, of pork, were the heaviest packages we had; they weighed 200 lbs. each, flour barrels 120 lbs., biscuit barrels 100 lbs. An experienced voyageur thinks nothing of a barrel of pork. I saw one fellow, a slight and by no means strong-looking man, carry *two* barrels of pork at the same time, and he asked for something else to be put on the top! He was a half-breed Indian from Fort William.

Another way of carrying the heavy pork-barrels was by means of a kind of hand-barrow made of two small poles (which are easily cut anywhere in the woods) and united by two slings made of 2-inch rope; the poles are run through the loops, and the barrel rests on the centre of the rope-slings. The men used to walk between the poles, the ends of which they held in their hands; and to ease the strain from their arms (which would otherwise have been very great), they used to fasten their portage straps to the poles, letting the broad parts rest across their shoulders, much in the same way as a milkman's wooden yoke, or as sedan-chairs used to be carried in former times in England. Colonel Wolseley had a number of these rope-slings constructed before leaving Prince Arthur's Landing, and issued to each boat. They were very generally adopted, and found to answer admirably, except that it took two men to carry a pork barrel instead of one man. However, they were only used for the heavy barrels and for the arm-chests.

It took us nearly the whole day getting our boat and stuff across this portage; we were new to the work, and the heat, being very great, rendered the

labour all the more severe.   It was half-past six in
the evening before we got away, but the excessive
beauty of the calm summer evening more than re-
paid us for the heat of the day.   By the aid of the
chart we found the way without difficulty.   Kashaboiwe Lake is about nine miles long, and studded
with beautifully-wooded islands.   We had got out
of the burnt region; and as the light gig pulled
quickly along, the calm beauty of the scene was
reflected back in wondrous perfection by the mirror-
like waters of the lake.   Not a sound but the
measured dip of the oars broke the perfect stillness
that reigned through these primeval woods, and we
forebore from conversation as if fearful that a human
voice would break the magic spell.   Each little
point and headland that we passed opened out new
beauties from Nature's inexhaustible treasure-house,
till the gathering shades of night warned us to look
out for a place to camp on.   We soon found a spot
on a pretty little island, where the lodge poles of an
Indian wigwam marked a favourite camping-ground
of these children of the woods, and leaving the men
to make a fire and cook our humble repast, D—— and
I jumped into the lake and increased our appetites
for supper by a refreshing swim.   We had two tents;
but only pitched one to take shelter in, in case of

rain. We all preferred bivouacking in the open air,
and after a composing pipe, wrapped in our blankets,
with our feet to the fire, and the blue vault of heaven
with its myriad stars for our roof, we soon fell
asleep, "far from the busy hum of men," with the
happy consciousness that a hard day's work

"Had earned a night's repose :"

such a sleep as would be envied by the toiling
millions of our crowded cities.

An hour's row in the freshness of the early morning brought us to the "Height of Land" Portage,
leading into Lac des Mille Lacs. Between this
Lake and Kashaboiwe Lake lies the high land
forming the watershed between Hudson's Bay and
the Gulf of St. Lawrence, Lac des Mille Lacs discharging its waters into the former, and Kashaboiwe
Lake into the latter. Between these two lakes is a
space of about two miles, but by taking advantage
of a small lake, called "Summit Pond," the distance
can be reduced considerably. Passing up a narrow
creek choked with weeds, and so shallow that we
had to jump out and wade and drag the boat through,
we got into Summit Pond, about a half mile long,
at the western end of which was the portage path.

Here we found two brigades hard at work. The

portage was 1,900 yards long and very severe, but by dividing it into two parts both brigades were able to work at the same time, one working on the far end, the other on the near end. For this purpose a broad road ten feet wide had to be cut through the woods, and trees laid down at intervals of about three feet as skids or rollers, on which the boats were dragged over on their keels to keep them from the rocky ground. The best trees for this purpose are the American poplars which happily abound in this sterile land. Whatever trees are used should be green and have a smooth bark; after rain or heavy dew there was a perceptible difference in the labour of dragging the boats; the wet made the bark slippery and the boats would then go over as if on greased rollers. On steep ground it was necessary to keep the skids in their places by driving strong wooden pegs into the ground alongside of them. After a little experience we found that on arriving at a portage it was always best to take the boat over first, whilst we were comparatively fresh, and the provisions afterwards.

The plan we adopted, and by which we found that the greatest amount of power could be got out of our crew, was as follows: four men tied their portage straps to the tow-line, two and two, the

other four tied theirs to the seats of the gig, two on
each side, at the stem and stern, to keep her on an
even keel ; the tow-line (made of four-inch rope)
was fastened to a hole made in the keel of the gig
near her fore-foot, which enabled the men pulling in
front to lift her nose over the skids ; then, with a
" yo-heave-oh," all pulled together with a will, each
man doing his utmost.   It was hard work even with
our light gig with only eight men, but some of the
large heavy boats required thirty or forty men to
get them up steep places.   This Height of Land
Portage was very trying to the men, some of the
boats having no less than twenty-three or twenty-four
barrels of pork in them besides other provisions in
proportion, and the labour of going backwards and
forwards so constantly with heavy loads was very
severe.   To lighten it, Captain Wallace of the 60th
improvised a rough sledge, cut out of a tree
where two branches of a similar size forked
out ; on this sledge eight or ten barrels could
be put at a time and dragged over the rollers, but
after a while it was given up, for the weight of the
sledge itself, which was necessarily made of green
wood, added much to the labour, and it was requisite
to have a man on each side of the sledge with a
lever to lift the nose of the sledge over the rollers.

Subsequently a few of the light carts belonging to the Transport Service were brought on to these first two portages and were of the greatest assistance, but they did not arrive until after the regulars had passed on. Some of the brigades were two and three days getting over this portage, working from morning to night, and the excessive severity of the labour began to tell upon the men.

CROSSING A PORTAGE.

The way in which all ranks worked, officers and men alike, was beyond all praise. The officers vied with their men in carrying heavy loads, and apart from the respect with which the officers were treated a stranger could not have told an officer from a private. Their dress was much the same: sleeves rolled up to the elbows; arms, neck, and hands as

brown as berries; loose flannel shirts open at the
throat, a pair of very dirty duck trowsers tucked
into mocassins, and a straw hat or red woollen
night-cap to crown all; little remnants of uniform
to be seen anywhere, except occasionally an odd
forage cap or two. The men had in most cases
patched the seats of their trowsers, which soon got
worn out by continual rowing, with pieces of canvas
from empty biscuit bags or flour bags, and presented
thereby a most comical appearance. Up early,
hard at work all day, rowing or portaging, from
five A.M. to eight P.M. with a short interval for
breakfast and dinner, nothing to eat but salt pork
and biscuit, nothing to drink but tea, they yet
looked as healthy and cheery as possible; and when
they reached Fort Frances, there was not a sick
man amongst them—they had no time to be sick.

The scale of daily rations laid down for the
troops, officers and men alike, was as follows: 1 lb.
of biscuit, 1 lb. of salt pork, 1 oz. of tea, 2 ozs. of
sugar, $\frac{1}{3}$ pint of beans, or $\frac{1}{4}$ lb. pound of preserved
potatoes, and on these the men did as hard work as
has ever been done by the men of any army. The
meat ration was undoubtedly rather meagre for
men doing such hard work, and $1\frac{1}{2}$ lbs. per day
would not have been too much. But as the troops

had to pass through a dreary wilderness of rocks, trees, and water, where no supplies of any description (except a few fish) could be procured, and as every ounce of food had to be carried on their own backs, an addition to the meat ration would have caused a very considerable addition to the weight to be carried over the portages, and therefore a delay to the expedition. The men were constantly wet through, wet sometimes for days together,— thoroughly done up by the severe labour of rowing, poling, tracking, and portaging; yet they were always well and cheery, and never seemed to feel the absence of spirituous liquors. This fact speaks for itself. I trust that the time has come when the issue of a spirit ration to a British army in the field will be for ever totally abolished. The men do not want it—they are better without it— better in every way. Throughout the Red River Expedition the absence of spirituous liquors was marked by an almost total absence of crime, as well as by the wonderful good health and spirits of the men. I do not hesitate to say that, had a spirit ration been issued, the results would have been very different. Take the case of trappers and lumberers in Canada, men who do harder work than any other class of men in the world; they live on bread, pork,

sugar and tea. If any one doubts the severity of
the work they perform, let him take an axe and go
and chop down trees for ten minutes, and he will
find that even in the coldest weather the perspira-
tion will pour from him. Lumberers will tell you
themselves, that they had rather not have whiskey
when they are chopping in the woods, and these
men are no teetotallers ; as soon as they get back to
their homes, they get drunk on whiskey. I know of
an instance in the Crimea where a fine young fellow,
a promising young sergeant, was tried by court-
martial and broken for being drunk in the trenches,
and it was proved at the court-martial that he had
drunk nothing but the double allowance of spirits
which was at that time issued to our men. Can
anything be stronger evidence than this of the
positive evil of the spirit ration?   How many
men too in the Crimea were tried for getting at the
keg of liquor in the trenches, which always had to
be kept under a sentry, and was a constant temp-
tation to the men and to the sentry himself? I
admit that, in a country where fuel is scarce, it
is difficult always to get wood to make the fire
necessary for tea ; but this should be provided by
the Commissariat, and the money and transport
saved by the absence of liquor would go a long

way towards supplying the fuel requisite for the
tea.   There is nothing that is so refreshing when
a man is thoroughly wet and tired as a good warm
cup of tea or coffee: it is fifty times as good as
brandy, rum, or whiskey.   The latter only warm
you up for a time and leave you colder than ever,
but the effect of tea or coffee lasts much longer and
leaves no vacuum behind it.   There may be medical
men in our army who would oppose the non-issue
of spirits; it was so with the Red River Expedition : some of the medical men asserted that it was a
mistake, that it would never do—but the result was
a most perfect triumph for tea ; and should the
same system ever be tried, as I hope and trust it
will in the next European war in which England
has to engage, I feel confident that the result would
be the same.   Not a man of the Red River Force
touched a drop of alcoholic or fermented liquor the
whole way from Shebandowan to Fort Garry, except
he was ill and received it from the store of medical
comforts, and there was positively no sickness and
a total absence of crime, combined with the utmost
cheerfulness and good humour, while the work performed stands wholly unrivalled for its unusual
nature as well as its severity.

The men soon get reconciled to the absence of

liquor, and appreciate the value of tea as a substitute, as the following anecdote will show. One day we were hauling our boat over a portage; it was the middle of the day and very hot, the portage was steep, and it was hard work. Some of the Colonel's crew of Iroquois came up to help us, to my great delight, for we were pretty well done, when a sudden jolt of the boat splashed up a little tea out of a big can that was in the stern-sheets. "Let's stop and have a drink," said some one. No sooner said than done. The big can, which held a couple of gallons, was soon emptied, though the tea was quite hot. The men crowded round, fearful lest they should be too late to get a drop; had it been beer or whiskey, they could not have shown a greater anxiety or gulped it down with more satisfaction. "By Jove! that's capital, puts new life into one," said one of my crew, a 60th man. "Yes," I replied, "better than all the beer in the world." "Well, sir, I really think it is," was his answer—and so it was. In hot weather cold tea is a most refreshing and stimulating beverage; and in cold or wet weather, who has a word to say against a delightful cup of warm tea?

But to return from this digression. We were nearly the whole of this day, the 23rd, getting

across this long portage, and it was late in the
evening before the gig was loaded and ready to
start again. The route here leads nearly due
north to about the centre of Lac des Mille Lacs,
and then turns westward along the old canoe
route. We had great difficulty in finding the way,
and at last camped for the night on a little island
full of wild roses *and* mosquitoes, utterly uncertain
of our whereabouts. Lac des Mille Lacs is a large
sheet of water about thirty miles long and six to
ten broad, and should rather be called Lac des
Mille Iles, so studded is its surface with islands.
These islands are of a peculiar nature. What looks
to be one enormous island at a little distance re-
solves itself on a nearer approach to an infinity
of small ones, which, separated only by narrow
channels, overlap and fit into one another like the
pieces of a Chinese puzzle, so that the traveller
may wander on from one little lake to another,
for miles. Hence the name given to it by the
Canadian voyageurs. Even the guides frequently
lose themselves for a time, and the only safe way
is to steer a course by compass, which our maps
were sufficiently accurate to enable us to do. The
scenery is wonderfully pretty, but the shores are
quite unfit for settlement, as there is but little

surface soil or moss spreading over the underlying rock. In some parts granitic dome-shaped rocks are numerous, and towards the western end, where the lake narrows on approaching Baril Portage, gneissoid hills and islands show a well-defined stratification dipping north. Exposures of white quartz called "Sail Rocks," from the resemblance they bear to the sails of distant boats, are frequent at the western extremity of the lake. Here and there the hills bear pine of fair dimensions, but as a rule the timber is very poor, and scarcely anything worth cutting for lumber purposes was to be seen anywhere along our route. Almost all the brigades lost their way for a few hours on this most beautiful but perplexing lake; but the canoe containing the *Globe* correspondent wandered about for two days amongst the islands, and eventually returned to the Height of Land Portage to wait for a guide.

Frightfully bullied all night by the mosquitoes, D—— and I were glad enough to get up early next morning and resume our search for the portage, which we at length hit off, arriving there about eleven o'clock. The distance from the last portage to Baril Portage is estimated at twenty miles, but we must have toiled over many miles more. Baril Portage is about 350 yards long, with a high hill in the centre, like a hog's back or a barrel; hence the name. We found D and E brigades of the 60th on this portage, and by the kind help of some of the men we got our boat up the steep hill and safely launched on the other side in Baril Lake. The day was fine and warm, not too hot, the heat being tempered with a pleasant breeze from the west, against which we beat up Baril Lake, a long narrow sheet of water about eight and a half miles in length. Spying a little headland jutting out from the north shore with a charming little bay on each side, we camped there for the night, and had here one of the jolliest little camps of many very jolly ones; we stopped rather earlier than usual, in order to set our net across a tempting little bay, for we were getting tired of our salt diet and longed for some fresh fish to supplement the salt pork. D—— and I made our beds on a spring mattress of Nature's own designing, two or three feet deep of the most beautiful moss, on which we slept the sleep of the just till 3.30 A.M. next morning, when awaking with the first flush of daylight we took a plunge in the lake whilst the men made a fire and boiled water for tea. We kept early hours, truly, regulating ourselves pretty much by the sun. As we

ate our biscuit and drank a warm cup of the liquid
"that cheers but not inebriates," we saw four or
five canoe-loads of Indians paddling down the lake
about 500 yards from us. They must have seen
the smoke of our camp-fire, but did not pay us
a visit, at which we rejoiced greatly, for these
Indians are sad mendicants, and we had no food
to spare, to give them. The result of our night's
fishing was disappointing; there was no fear of the
net breaking from the "multitude of fishes," for
not a solitary one did we capture.

A half-hour's row brought us to Brulé Portage,
and by 8.45 A.M. we had got our boat and stuff
across, cooked and eaten breakfast, and were ready
for a fresh start. The heavy dew of the night
before had made the skids slippery, and the gig
was hauled over with little trouble. Brulé Portage
is 500 yards long; the path winds round the foot
of a steep hill 200 feet high, and is not unlike a
path through an English wood. The vegetation
was very luxuriant, though young; the remains
of the dead trunks of half-burnt trees, lying hidden
by a profuse growth of brushwood, indicated the
origin of the name. The second growth consisted
chiefly of black cherry, birch, white and black alder,
and a thick undergrowth of hazel-nut.

Embarking again at the foot of the portage path, forty-seven feet below Baril Lake, we descended a winding rushy stream opening out into a continuation of lovely lakes and lakelets, connected together by rapid streams and dull quiet creeks, fringed with cedar and spruce, and covered with thick beds of the beautiful white lily and its golden-hued companion. The scenery was very beautiful, though somewhat monotonous. This part of the route is called by the Indians "Lake Windegoostigon," which I believe means, a series of lakes.

Coming at last to a shallow rapid stream, we had to get out and walk through the woods, whilst the two voyageurs took the boat down : we followed it for about three miles and then came to some pretty falls, round which was the new portage path, 400 yards long. Here we found Colonel Feilden and the three leading brigades. They were occupied, when we arrived, in cutting out the road and laying down skids, an operation quickly performed by the voyageurs. The old portage, which we had avoided by coming down this stream, is two miles long and a truly dreadful portage. It is nothing but a continued series of climbing up and down steep and rocky hills, and the labour of portaging everything over it would have been dreadful to

contemplate. It would have taken each brigade
from three to four days of the most severe labour.
The new portage path descends a very steep hill,
down which the stream finds its way, a little to the
east of the path in a series of very pretty cascades.

Having caught up with the leading brigades, the
gig was now able to take it easily. Next morning,
the 26th, we embarked again on the same stream,
which now became deep and sluggish, too deep to
pole and too narrow for rowing, but very pretty ;
its banks fringed with alder, tamarack, and pitch-
pine, and occasional larger trees of white and red
pine. As we dropped lazily down with the current,
enjoying the luxury of a morning pipe, an occasional young partridge would flutter away through
the bushes, scared at our approach ; numerous
pigeons flitted about, and looked down at us from
the lofty pines with wondering eyes, evidently un-
used to the "human face divine." They presented
the most tempting shots, and made our mouths
water with delicious but tantalizing visions of
pigeon-pie, but alas! there was no shot-gun in
the gig ; so we had to amuse ourselves by scaring
them from their perches by a loud shout, and then
presenting imaginary guns at them as they flew
away. This stream has so many sharp turns and

twists that although in a straight line it is only two miles from point to point, yet following the windings the distance must be fully ten or eleven miles. To give an idea of the way in which it wriggles and bends about, an officer told me that about ten minutes after leaving the portage, when he thought he had gone at least half a mile, he missed his purse, which he recollected having left on the ground near his tent. Just at that moment he heard a voice hailing them, and found that it came from a man belonging to a brigade at work on the portage, who had wandered away a little from the path. He sent the man back for the purse, which was found on the spot indicated, not more than 200 *yards off!*

This stream connects Lake Windegoostigon with French Lake, a pretty circular basin 1½ miles in diameter, surrounded by low hills timbered with an extensive forest of red pine. The temperature on this western side of the watershed is much milder than to the eastward of it, the level of the country sinking steadily as we proceed, French Lake being 150 feet below Lac des Mille Lacs. On the shores of this lake a humming-bird was seen for the first time.

Going on through two smaller lakes, connected by

a very pretty river about 1½ miles long, we came out into Lake Kaogassikok, or Pickerel Lake, a fine sheet of water thirteen miles long by two to four broad, at the western extremity of which is Portage des Pins. The timber on this portage was the finest we had yet seen, many really splendid specimens of white and red pine crowning the portage, and looking proudly down upon a young growth of the sugar-maple. A row of a mile across Doré Lake brought us to the next portage, called Deux Rivières, 750 yards long, and very steep and rocky. On first walking across this portage, it seemed as if it would be almost impossible to lay down rollers for the boats up and down such steep hills, but old Ignace and his crew of Iroquois (ten men), assisted by the voyageurs of the three brigades, made a capital road by five o'clock the next evening. At one spot they cut down two huge red pines, large enough to be the spars of a big ship, and, laying them lengthwise, put skids across on notches cut in the pines, and thus made a capital bridge across a ravine, lessening the ascent very much.

This afternoon, the 28th, Colonel Wolseley came up in his canoe, accompanied by Mr. Irvine, and the gig thenceforth joined the Head-Quarter camp.

As Colonel Wolseley had passed the different
brigades one after the other, he found that they
had had considerable trouble at many places in
finding the right road, the numerous deep bays
which in many of these lakes branch off in every
direction rendering it very difficult to avoid losing
the right track. It is most disheartening for the
men to find, when they get to the end of one of
these bays, that they have come eight or ten
miles out of the way and have all that distance
to row back again. Consequently, when there
is the slightest doubt about the route no one
cares to push on quickly, when doing so may be
leading them a long distance astray. Colonel
Wolseley, therefore, with the canoe and gig from
this point up to Fort Frances, kept well ahead
of the leading detachment, and "blazed" trees
at every turn of the track or doubtful point.

For the benefit of the uninitiated, I may mention that "blazing" a tree is scoring it with
an axe, so that the white inner wood makes a
plain and distinct mark. An Indian, as he walks
through a wood, will "blaze" a tree here and
there on either side of his path, generally ten
to twenty yards apart, with one stroke of his
axe, so dexterously, as not to shorten the pace

of his long springy stride. But our "blazes" were very different; we used to select a group of conspicuous trees at a point where the route turned to the right or left, and a couple of men would spring ashore with axes, lop off the lower branches, and strip the bark off for several feet, thus making a mark visible for a mile or more. After this plan had been adopted, the brigades in rear got on much better.

From Deux Rivières Portage, the route leads through a narrow winding channel, overgrown with rushes and lilies, into Sturgeon Lake, the most beautiful of the many beautiful lakes yet passed. The sudden contraction of the lake into a river breadth for a few yards amongst islands, and its abrupt opening out into wide expanses of water, with deep and gloomy bays stretching into the dark forest as far as the eye could reach, offered a picture of ever-changing beauty. Half-way up this lake we met a large North-West canoe, manned by Iroquois Indians, and found that it contained Mr. Simpson, M.P. for Algoma, and Mr. Pither. The latter gentleman had been living at Fort Frances for some months past, having been sent by the Ottawa Government to inform the Indians of the intention of Government

to send troops through their country, and to arrange
with them for right of way. He had reached
Fort Frances in the month of March, after a long
and toilsome journey on snow-shoes across the
lakes. Mr. Simpson had been sent up subsequently
to conclude a treaty with them, Mr. Pither
having paved the way. Both gentlemen turned
back and accompanied us to Fort Frances, after
some little difficulty with their crew, who did not
like to see the head of their canoe turned westward again.

Sturgeon Lake empties itself into Lac la Croix,
through Sturgeon River, about 18 miles long,
with numerous falls and heavy rapids, about
which we had heard such gloomy accounts in
Ottawa from those who professed to know the
route. These rapids are four in number, and close
together. The boats were taken down by the
Iroquois without injury, the only one damaged
being one that was allowed to be taken down by
the regular Canadian voyageurs. The celebrated
guide Ignace and his crew were invaluable at
this work, and Colonel Wolseley left them at the
rapids to take the boats of the succeeding brigades
down too. Portage de l'Isle, the last of several portages on Sturgeon River, is a very pretty portage

on an island, as its name implies. The river divides into two channels and falls over a ledge of rock in the most picturesque cascades.

Having now two crews of Indians besides the gig, we tried to help on the leading detachment by cutting out the portage roads for them,—a proceeding which, with such experienced axe-men, took a wonderfully short time. It is perfectly astonishing to see the way in which trees of large dimensions fall before the axe of the backwoodsman; they appear to be swept away like corn before the reaper; anything under 18 inches in diameter stands but a very few blows from the heavy chopping-axe. In cutting down a tree, an Indian or backwoodsman follows a regular system, and does not go hacking at it all round as an inexperienced man does; he makes a clean wedge-shaped cut into it on the side on which he wishes it to fall, the end of the wedge being as near a right angle as possible. When he has thus cut about half-way through the tree, a small nick cut on exactly the opposite side causes it to fall in a line with the edge of the wedge-shaped cut. In this way, any tree that is vertical, or nearly so, can be made to fall in any required direction, unless there should be a strong wind blowing, when it is difficult to

K

make it fall against the wind. One of our party
seemed to have a most extraordinary faith in the
skill of an Indian, and his power of making a tree
fall in any direction, and caused much amusement
and chaff by his arguments in support of his theory.
He was at last confronted with a tree that was
leaning at an angle of about 60° with the ground,
and told to make that fall the contrary way. He
requested one of the Indians to do so, but the man
shook his head and laughed, and our friend had
to give up his pet theory; and I think his faith in
the powers of an Indian was much shaken from
that day. I remember, however, one case in which
an Indian showed great dexterity in cutting down
a tree. It was at the camp on the Matawan River.
A tall and branchless pine was leaning over Colonel
Wolseley's tent in a very dangerous way, threatening
to fall and crush the occupant on the first heavy
breeze of wind. An Indian was summoned to cut
it down, and after great care and judgment, he
made the tree fall between the tent and the mess-
table with great nicety; a couple of feet one
way or the other, and it would have fallen on
the tent or on the table. He cut his wedge with
mathematical accuracy, and just as the tree cracked
and bent to its fall a couple of swiftly-dealt blows

with the back of the axe on one side of the trunk made it fall just clear of the table.

From Portage de l'Isle a few miles further brought us to Lac la Croix, a long and broad sheet of water, so named by some Jesuit missionaries many years ago, who erected two large wooden crosses on conspicuous islands at the western end of the lake. The crosses have disappeared, but the lake retains the name. The Indians call it "Nequaquon." The old canoe route turns off at the north-western end and follows the Rivière Maligne into Lake Namekan, but this route was pronounced very dangerous for the big boats, the river being full of rapids and sunken rocks and long portages. Mr. Donald Smith's canoe was twice broken during his recent descent of this river, although manned by the best Iroquois. We therefore followed the lake to its western end, and then turned south for a few miles into Loon Lake, and made a bend round, coming into Namekan Lake and joining the old canoe route again. By this detour we avoided the dangerous rapids of the Rivière Maligne.

On one of the portages on Loon Lake we came across some Indians, three old women and some children. One of the old women was the most

hideous old hag that it is possible to imagine,
skinny, wrinkled, withered, bent, clothed in rags ,
and tatters, and very old.   Mr. Pither informed
us that she was a *cannibal;* that is to say,
she had been one of a party some winters previously who had been starved into eating human
flesh.   We gave these poor creatures a little flour
and biscuit, which made them quite happy and
contented, and the old hag went up and begged
from the men the water in which their pork had
been boiled.   One of our party that morning was
a lady (the only one that accompanied the expedition), who had bravely followed her husband and
shared his canoe through all the perils and fatigues
of the journey.   The old hag seemed lost in wonder
at the sight of this lady, and truly the contrast
between the two was so wonderful, that it was
hard to believe that they could be beings of the
same nature, hard to realize that the difference
between them was only owing to the human
agency of education and civilization.   The old
hag was such a horrid object to look at that we
were glad to make our escape from her.

Crossing Lake Namekan, we came to Portage
Nu, the last before Fort Frances.   This really
consists of two portages, with a narrow sluggish

stream between. We had just finished cutting
out the path and laying the skids when Colonel
Feilden's detachment came up.   It was quite a
sight to see them arrive at a portage, to see the
men spring out, unload the boats, and haul them
over, the crews vying with each other as to who
should get everything over first.   No delay or
hesitation : as soon as a barrel was landed from
the boat, somebody seized it, tied his portage
strap round it, and off to the other end of the
portage, *running* back to get another load. The
men by this time were thoroughly up to the
work, and thought nothing of a portage under.
half a mile in length. Bare Portage was found
worthy of its name,—bare and swampy, full of
mosquitoes and black flies which annoyed us
much : the stream, too, was so full of leeches that
it was impossible to bathe in it. We were glad
to get away from it after a not very pleasant
night, delighted to think we had a fair stretch of
46 miles of open water without a portage.

At the entrance into Rainy Lake we met a
strong north-westerly gale, against which we could
make no headway, and were obliged to take
shelter on an island, where we were detained all
day by the violence of the wind. Some of us

were not sorry at this detention, for the island was covered with a wonderful profusion of the largest and finest blue-berries, as large as cherries, as delicious as grapes, and with a bloom like a peach, and no stones inside. We ate them until we could not stand, and then we lay down and ate them again, and fell asleep to wake up and attack them again! We filled every spare vessel we had with gallons of blue-berries; we had blue-berry jam, blue-berry bread, and blue-berries in every conceivable shape possible to our limited culinary skill and appliances. The Indians live on blue-berries in the summer, but until we came across this island, I had no idea what a blue-berry could be, and was formerly rather inclined to look contemptuously on them.

Amongst the vegetable products of this region is a plant called Poisoned Ivy or Ground Ivy. The leaf is shaped like the hazel-leaf, but not quite so deep in colour, and is smoother on the surface and along the edge. The plant is perennial, about a foot high, and bears a pale yellowish flower in the early spring: the leaves grow in triplets, and are broad and long. If the leaf is plucked and rubbed against the face or hands, or if a man run over it with bare feet and crush it,

the poison makes the part touched swell like ery-
sipelas ; a cluster of little pimples appear which
turn into blisters, and the discharge from which
will communicate the poison to other parts of the
body. The attack lasts nine days, although it
frequently leaves symptoms about the body for
months afterwards. The irritation and pain are
excessive. Both Mr. Simpson and Mr. Pither
had suffered dreadfully from its effects, and stated
that during the attack they could only find relief
by sitting in cool water for hours together. It is
not known to all the Iroquois, though the Ojibeways
know it well. Mr. Pither told us of an Indian
who, being sceptical as to its effects, rubbed his face
with it. Two days afterwards his face and head
were so swollen that his features were scarcely
distinguishable. He could not see out of his eyes,
and was in great pain. Some people are said to
be able to handle it with impunity, and this is the
only way by which one can account for the fact
that it abounds all over the country, and that
Indians camp frequently in the midst of it, when
their children would necessarily touch it constantly.

Next day the same head winds delayed us,
and we could only make progress in the very
early morning and late in the evening. Rainy

Lake is an enormous sheet of water, the largest we had yet passed through, being about 50 miles long by 30 to 40 broad. Its shores present a sterile and hopeless aspect; the timber is very poor, and bleached and naked rocks are visible for miles together. It is about 420 feet above the level of Lake Superior, and is 225 miles west of that lake. Its waters are clear but warm, and not very deep, and flow into Lake of the Woods by a magnificent river, 80 miles long, called Rainy River, which issues from its western extremity. The canoe route takes a nearly west course through about 38 miles of the lake.

On the morning of the 4th August, after two days' detention by contrary winds, we were under way again at 4.15 A.M., and soon got to the end of the lake and commenced to descend Rainy River. The aspect of the country here changes entirely, as if by magic; the banks of the river are low and alluvial, and covered with a dense second growth, and the land has all the appearance of great fertility. A rapid run of three miles down the river brought us to the long-expected half-way house, Fort Frances; and glad indeed were we to see signs of the abode of man after the desolate and inhospitable region we had passed through.

CHAPTER VIII.

FORT FRANCES.

FORT FRANCES, one of the Hudson's Bay Company's posts, is situated on the right bank of Rainy River, about three miles below the lake, in lat. 48° 35′ N., long. 93° 40′ W. It consists of a collection of wooden one-storied block-houses, surrounded by a palisading, and is built on a position of some natural strength and of great beauty. Just opposite to it are the falls, round which is the portage. These falls are very lovely. The whole body of water of Rainy River, some 300 yards wide, tumbles over a ledge of rock about 22 feet in height, in a volume of spray and mist, with a roar audible for many miles. Below, the river glides tranquilly along between high wooded banks, in a straight stretch of a mile and a half. The view from the fort is very charming, combining all

the essentials of picturesque beauty except that of
mountain scenery. There has been at one time a
good deal of cleared land round the post, but
much of it has been allowed to return to its primitive wildness, and is becoming covered with a
scrubby, second growth. There is capital pasture-
land, the grass being green and luxuriant, as fine
as is to be seen in any part of Canada. To our
eyes, wearied with the monotonous sameness of the
barren and inhospitable region we had lately passed
through, this green and fertile oasis in the midst
of the desert of rock, forest, and water, was like
a glimpse of the Promised Land.

Mr. McKenzie, the Hudson's Bay Company's
official in charge of the post, was most civil and
obliging, giving up a room in his house for the use
of Colonel Wolseley and the Head-quarter staff, and
allowing us to have the run of our teeth in his
garden, so that during our stay of five days we
revelled in green peas, young potatoes, and cabbages,
most agreeable antidotes to the scorbutic ten-
dencies of salt pork. The luxury, too, of having a
chair to sit on, and a table to write at, is not to be
despised. Mr. McKenzie had a few acres of wheat,
barley, and Indian corn, all of which looked
remarkably well; the wheat was ready for the

sickle, and the grain fine and full. Wheat is sown here about the last week in April, and takes about ninety days to come to maturity. Potatoes, sown about the 8th of May, were fit for the table when we arrived. There were no pigs, sheep, or fowls, but about twenty head of cattle, three of which we bought for the use of the troops, so that the men as they passed through got a meal of fresh meat. The winter lasts nearly seven months, so that cattle require a vast quantity of hay during the long, weary winter months. Snow falls to a depth of about four feet, and indeed in most respects the climate of this section of the country is very similar to that of Lower Canada.

All along the banks of Rainy River is a strip of alluvial soil, which on the right or British bank extends inland for a width of from half a mile to ten miles, where it is bounded by a vast swamp joining the shores of Rainy Lake to those of Lake of the Woods. This swamp was described by Mr. Pither as consisting of a springy, moveable surface, overlying a deposit of peat, through which a pole might be pushed to a depth of thirty feet without reaching the bottom. It is covered with a growth of scrubby bush, interspersed with islands of small pine, and follows the windings of the river. At

the back of Fort Frances, the fertile wooded belt
is only half a mile wide.

Rainy River forms the boundary line between
British and American territory.

When we arrived at the fort on the morning of
the 4th of August, Mr. McKenzie sent down a
cart, which he had constructed expressly for the
use of the expedition, to help the men over the
portage round the falls. This cart was of such a
peculiar nature that it deserves a special description. It was made of wood throughout, not a nail
or piece of any metal whatever being employed in
its construction. The wheels, about 18 inches in
diameter, were composed of solid blocks of wood
nearly a foot thick, and rounded with an axe.
The axle-tree was literally a large "tree" fitted into
the wheels; and the body of the vehicle, which
scarcely stood more than twelve inches from the
ground, was similarly made, and was only large
enough to hold a very small amount of stuff. The
"thing" was drawn by an ox, harnessed between
a pair of enormous shafts, with a saddle, collar,
and traces like a horse. This primitive vehicle
caused much amusement to the men, who dubbed
it "Our Transport Service," though I believe it was
a source of considerable pride to its maker.   I

regret to say that it very soon came to pieces, the fastenings being only of buffalo hide or wood.

At the entrance to Rainy River we met Lieutenant Butler, of the 69th Regiment, who had just arrived that morning from Fort Garry. He had been sent from Canada by the Lieutenant-General as an intelligence officer, and had visited Duluth, Marquette, and other towns on the south shore of Lake Superior, to see if there were any chance of the threatened Fenian raid on our communications actually taking place. Those towns were known to be full of a large Irish element, who had openly declared their intention to obstruct the progress of the expedition in every possible way. From thence Lieutenant Butler had gone to St. Paul's in Minnesota, and then boldly made his way straight to Fort Garry, where his arrival caused much excitement amongst the rebel authorities. His life was not considered safe in the settlement, so after receiving a visit from "President" Riel, in which, I believe, the advisability of an early departure was pretty plainly hinted to him, he procured a boat by the aid of some of the loyal people, and made his way up the Winnipeg River to meet Colonel Wolseley. He brought news from Red River to the 24th July, and described the condition of affairs there as full of anarchy and confusion, the French and English settlers mutually afraid of one another, and both parties in dread of an Indian outbreak, and Riel very anxious about an amnesty. They knew nothing in Red River of the whereabouts of the expedition, which Riel declared would never reach Fort Garry. Most people seemed to think that, if no amnesty were forthcoming, Riel would show fight and oppose the entrance of the troops. Mr. Butler brought some good boatmen with him, who were afterwards very useful as guides and steersmen for the Winnipeg River.

The tribe of Indians who inhabit the wild region extending from Lake Superior to the banks of the Red River and Lake Winnipeg is the Ojibeway or Chippewa. They are divided into several branches, but all speak the same language, the poetic tongue of "Hiawatha." They are wood Indians, and differ materially from the Indians of the plains, the Sioux and Crees, with whom they have a long-standing feud. Though not so warlike a race as the plain Indians, they yet occasionally go out to fight their enemies the Sioux, and have old traditions of enmity against the Iroquois. The latter speak a language totally distinct from the Chippewas, not a mere difference of dialect, but a language as unlike the Chippewa as English is unlike French. They have no settled abodes, frequenting chiefly the alluvial valleys of the large rivers, such as the Kaministiquia and Rainy rivers, and are to be found roving in their little canoes all over the lakes and streams of the country.

Large numbers of them frequent the vicinity of Fort Frances for the sake of the sturgeon fishing in Rainy River, and assemble annually to the number of 500 or 600 to hold their great medicine ceremonies. When Mr. Simpson arrived at Fort Frances to make a treaty with them for right of way, they held a meeting to discuss the advisability of opposing the passage of the troops, but gave up the idea on being assured that it was quite impossible to do so. Although I do not think it possible that they could ever combine in any large numbers for such a purpose, yet there is no doubt that a hundred determined men might have inflicted tremendous loss on the troops with comparative impunity; for, thoroughly acquainted with the vast network of lakes, they could have fired on the boats as they passed through narrow channels, or blocked up the portages, and done much mischief in a variety of ways, while to have attempted to pursue them through the woods and lakes would

have been madness. They go about in the neatest
possible little birch-bark canoes, just large enough
to hold three men, and so light as to be portaged
by one man with ease for long distances. The men
are fine, tall fellows, with broad, heavy features
displeasing to our European eyes, though some of
them are good-looking enough: they wear their
hair confined round the forehead by a ribbon,
but plaited behind into two long tails hanging
down their backs; and with the exception of a
breech-cloth round the waist, their only garment is
a blanket, which they wear wrapped round them
like a Roman toga.

When we arrived at Fort Frances, we found only
about half-a-dozen lodges, though great numbers
had been there a month before. They waited a
long time for us to come, expecting presents of
flour, pork, and tobacco, but hope deferred had
made their stomachs sick, and hunger had driven
them off to their usual fishing avocations. Their
principal chief, Crooked Neck (a hideous old fellow,
so called from his head being all on one side), was
still there, and honoured us with a visit.

It was a novel and interesting scene; about a
dozen of them, clad in various-coloured blankets,
stalked into the room and shook hands with us all

round, then squatted on the floor in a semi-
circle, whilst one of their number stepped to the
front, accompanied by his "backer," and addressed
us in a very loud voice, with much gesticulation
and repetition. The pith of his speech, which was
a very long one, was that they were glad to be in
the presence of a big white Chief sent by their
Great Mother, the Queen, and that they would give
us the right of way, with use of wood and water,
through their land, for which privilege they de-
manded ten dollars a head annually for every man,
woman, and child, but that they would sell none
of their land, and wanted no white settlers to live
amongst them. Colonel Wolseley's reply, which
was very short, was that he was very glad to see
them, but had no concern with their lands, only
requiring a right of way through their country;
and that he was sorry he had no presents for them,
having only provisions enough for his own people.
We had a half-breed to interpret for us, who trans-
lated the Chippewa, into French, and very bad
French too. The pow-wow lasted some time, and
we were all getting rather bored and glad to get
rid of them, which we eventually did by shaking
hands again all round, and giving them some small
presents of flour and pork. The old chief, " Crooked

Neck," is a cunning old savage.   At their grand
medicine ceremonies held about a month before our
arrival, he appeared in a costume of his own, which
he evidently considered the height of Chippewa
fashion.   He was quite naked, with the exception
of a breech-cloth round his waist, but his body was
painted a bright yellow, and he had a brass ring
round his neck.   On this occasion he refused to
accept the presents that Mr. Simpson had brought
for him, such as gaudy red shirts and coats and
caps, just the thing to catch the eye of an Indian,
and please his fancy.   "Am I a pike," said he with
virtuous indignation, "to be caught with such a
bait as that?   Shall I sell my land for a bit of
red cloth ?   We will let the pale-faces pass through
our country, but we will sell them none of our
land, nor have any of them to live amongst us."

These Indians are polygamists, and marry as many
wives as they can afford to keep.   The women are
very ugly, except in extreme youth, and speedily
lose their good looks, and are old women at the age
of thirty.   They are excessively filthy in their
habits, their persons are covered with vermin, and
entirely innocent of soap and water.   Old " Crooked
Neck " had several wives of various degrees of dirt
and ugliness, only one of whom was at all good-

looking. She was a very young girl, and would
have been almost pretty had she been properly
" cleaned." The morality of the women is not of
a high order, which is not to be wondered at, considering the state of degradation in which they
are kept. Poor things! they are the slaves and
drudges of the men, who loaf about, or sit and
smoke at the doors of their lodges in lazy indolence,
whilst the women cut wood, draw water, cook, &c.
The men are too lazy even to fish, until hunger
compels them to do so.

Their wigwams are made of a number of poles
tied together at the top in the shape of a bell ;
round the bottom and nearly up to the top are
fastened strips of birch-bark or deer-skin, leaving
room for a doorway ; the top is left open to let out
the smoke of the fire which is lighted inside in
the middle ; the whole family, husband, wives and
children, live together in one lodge. When they
shift their camp, the poles are left standing for the
use of the next comer, or for themselves when they
return that way, but the strips of bark are rolled up
and carried by the women in their canoe. The man
always has a canoe to himself, in which he takes
nothing but his gun and blankets, and "paddles his
own canoe." The impedimenta of the party, the

household gods of the family, are taken by the squaws in their canoe. One's preconceived ideas of the North American Indian, as derived from the fascinating pages of Fenimore Cooper, or the romantic verses of the author of "Hiawatha," are rudely dispelled by the reality, and one is forced to doubt whether Longfellow ever saw much of the Chippewa Indian in his native wilds.

A day or two after our first audience with "Crooked Neck" we were favoured by a visit from another chief, whose name I forget, but who came from some distance to see the great Chief of the pale-faces, accompanied by two of his wives and a male attendant. This fellow's dress was most absurd. To begin with, he was half red and half black, like the "Perfect Cure," or a clown in a pantomime. His coat was an old military scarlet coatee, with epaulettes and tawdry old gold lace very much the worse for wear. The right half of this coat had been cut off and replaced by a portion of a black coat, also adorned with lace on the collar and cuffs. His shirt was scarcely long enough for decency, and terminated in deer-skin mocassins and leggings reaching to the knee, prettily worked with beads, and fringed with many-coloured tassels. Round his body, like a Roman toga, was wrapped a red blanket, which, when accidentally exposed or blown aside by the wind, left between his leggings and his shirt a "hiatus valdè deflendus!" He also wore a handsome kind of cross-belt, thrown over his right shoulder like a sash of the present day, embroidered heavily with beads. On his head was a high wide-awake hat, adorned with a green ribbon. His face was painted to match, the left side a bright red, the right its natural dark hue. When he turned suddenly round from left to right, the sudden change from red to black was most ludicrous, and made us laugh heartily. Otherwise, he was a fine-looking savage, and when one did not see the red half of his nose, rather good-looking. We had a pow-wow with him, which ended as usual by his shaking hands with us two or three times all round, and then making off with his plug of tobacco, highly delighted at the gift.

At the great medicine ceremonies which these Indians hold every summer at Fort Frances for the purpose of initiating candidates into the mysteries of medicine, they go through extraordinary orgies, not unlike the old Roman Saturnalia. Part of the ceremony consists in killing every white dog they can get hold of, boiling the flesh, and feasting on it. The men dress up in the most outlandish manner :

one fellow danced a scalp dance with nothing on but a frock-coat; another had his body white-washed as far as the waist, his left cheek painted green and the right blue, his ribs painted with black finger-marks as if he had been gripped in a deadly wrestle, his arms and feet painted to represent blood and bruises; in this hideous "attire" he danced a war dance, reciting his deeds of valour, and the scalps he had taken from the Sioux.

The candidates for "medicine-men" are taught the virtues of many wild roots and plants, in the use of which consists their only skill in curing disease. Of anatomy or surgery they know nothing. Some of these medicine-men know the uses of many deadly vegetable poisons, amongst which I was told of a plant the root of which possesses the horrible power of turning the complexion quite black. Mr. Pither pointed out to me a woman whom, he said, he had known as a young girl, at which time she was very pretty, and of comparatively a fair complexion. Some of this poison had been administered to her and had turned her quite black. Certainly, when I saw her, she was hideously black and ugly. They use also the root of the Sarsaparilla plant, the gold thread (good for ulcerated sore-throats), and the red willow, the bark of which makes a capital astrin-

gent, as I myself found by practical experience, for
one day, having strained my left wrist in rowing,
Mr. Pither gathered some of the red willow, removed the outer bark, and scraping the inner bark,
boiled it for about half an hour, and applied it to
the wrist, giving great relief.

The portage at Fort Frances, which is a large
cleared field covered with luxuriant grass, was
formerly used by the Indians as a burial-ground.
Some of the bodies were buried in the ground in
the usual way; on one of them, a child's grave,
which had been neatly fenced in by some sorrowing
mother to preserve it from desecration, I was much
touched at observing, carefully laid by the side of
the grave, a child's paddle and little toy canoe.
Human nature does not differ much all the world
over—

> " One touch of nature makes the whole world kin."

The bodies of the great chiefs are, however, not
buried in the ground, but placed in wooden boxes
and hung up on a framework six or seven feet above
the ground, suspended in mid-air, as it were. The
effluvium from these boxes soon becomes very great,
and as they are put up in the most conspicuous
places, they are particularly objectionable. " Have
I not my father's and my grandfather's bones ? "

said old "Crooked Neck" in his speech.   We saw a great deal *too much* of "Crooked Neck" during our stay at Fort Frances; he used to stalk about, his sole covering being a blanket wrapped round him, long matted hair hanging over his shoulders, which he was too lazy to plait into two tails in the usual manner, and confined round the forehead by a piece of greasy ribbon.   In this easy costume he would peer into our tents, or coolly walk into the room as we sat writing, evidently considering that the whole place belonged to him, and that *we* were only there on sufferance.   His lodge was close by, and D——— and I used to pass it every morning on our way to our matutinal plunge in the river.

When a chief is *buried* (not suspended in mid-air), it is the custom of the Chippewas to bury with him his gun and a kettle.   The Indians of the plains, besides the gun, kill over the grave the dead chief's favourite horse, in order that when he arrives at the happy hunting grounds, he may be ready, mounted and armed.   Is not this something like our own custom at a military funeral of leading the charger to the grave behind the coffin ?   The connection of ideas and customs on this point is at least curious, though I have heard that ours is derived from an old German custom.

Before Colonel Wolseley left Fort Frances, he saw the whole of the regular troops and the first two brigades of militia pass on. As they went through, each brigade left what surplus stores they had brought with them to form a depôt of supplies at Fort Frances. A hospital was established capable of accommodating thirty-six patients, and a field-oven was put up and a bakery started, by which means the rear brigades were served out with two days' fresh bread, a pleasant change after the hard biscuit. A company of the 1st Ontario Rifles was left as a garrison, and their camp was pitched on the grassy bank over the river close by the fort. Each brigade as it passed through also got rid of incompetent voyageurs, and out of six brigades twelve men were thus left behind, or an average of one-seventh, a high proportion, considering that they had already been freely weeded before leaving Shebandowan.

On the 5th August Mr. Monkman, a loyal English half-breed from Red River, arrived, bringing letters from the settlement to the 20th of July. During the troubles of the previous winter, Mr. Monkman had incurred the hatred of Riel's party for assisting the escape of Dr. Schultz; his life being in danger, he fled to Canada, crossing the dreary wilderness in the depth of winter on snow-shoes. He had been warmly received in Ontario, and had been presented to H.R.H. Prince Arthur, who had made him a present of some tobacco. He passed through Fort William in June 1870 on his way to Red River, and promised Colonel Wolseley to come out and meet him at Fort Frances at the latter end of July with the latest news from Red River, and with information regarding supplies and the feasibility of using the road from the north-west angle of Lake of the Woods for the transport of the troops. He nobly kept his promise, and brought letters from Bishop Macrae and others, also one from " Henry Prince," the chief of the Saulteux or Swampy Indians at Red River, full of loyalty and breathing dislike to Riel and his party. The refrain of all these letters was the same—" Come on as quickly as you can, for the aspect of affairs is serious, and an Indian outbreak is imminent." Mr. Monkman had entered the settlement from the north-west angle, following his old blazed line along a good sandy ridge to White Mouth River, till he reached Mr. Snow's road, where he narrowly escaped capture from an outlying party of Riel's men. He strongly advocated taking the troops through this line, as he said that very little labour would make the swamps

passable for carts, but other accounts did not agree
with this description, and Colonel Wolseley had had
too much already of *one* road to risk the success of
the expedition on *another* which he had not seen
himself, or through the eyes of a British officer.
Mr. Monkman also brought the pleasing intelligence
that six large Hudson's Bay boats had been sent up
the Winnipeg River, well manned by experienced
boatmen, to assist the expedition in descending the
dangerous rapids of that river. The expenses of
this had been defrayed by a subscription amongst
the loyal inhabitants, and the boats were accompanied by the Reverend Mr. Gardiner, an energetic
Presbyterian clergyman, who had been one of the
principal promoters of the undertaking and had
himself subscribed largely thereto.

Having carefully made every possible arrangement for supplying the brigades with guides across
the Lake of the Woods, Colonel Wolseley started
at daylight on the 10th August to catch Colonel
Feilden and the leading brigades before they reached
Fort Alexander.

CHAPTER IX.

At daylight on the 10th, Colonel Wolseley left
Fort Frances and resumed his journey in a bark
canoe manned by Iroquois, and the gig kept
company with its crew of soldiers. D—— and I
had got rid of our French-Canadian voyageur, who
was sick (a little sick of the hard work, too, perhaps),
and in his place had got a young Iroquois Indian
whose French name was "Baptiste." We soon
found the benefit of the exchange, for there was
not a smarter Indian in the whole expedition
than young "Ba'tiste," always cheery and good-
humoured, ready either to take an oar or a paddle,
and a capital fellow on a portage. Aided by the
current, which runs about $1\frac{1}{2}$ or 2 miles an hour,
we descended Rainy River easily and quickly,
making about $5\frac{1}{2}$ miles per hour on an average.

By one o'clock in the afternoon we had run
about 40 miles, and stopped for an hour for
dinner just at the foot of the second rapids.

The general course of this beautiful river is a
few degrees to the north of west for a distance
of 80 miles, following the windings of the river,
or about 60 miles in a direct line. Its breadth is
from 200 to 400 yards, though it becomes broader
near its junction with Lake of the Woods. The
navigation is unfortunately broken by the beautiful
falls at Fort Frances, but from that point to its
mouth, although there are two strong rapids, the
" Manitou " and " Long-sault," about half-way
down, yet these present no difficulty to the
passage of a powerful steamer. The banks of the
river are very beautiful ; we passed groves of
basswood and sturdy oaks, standing in grassy
park-like expanses, and open glades stretching
away into a forest of elm, ash, and balsam-poplar.
The grass was very green and luxuriant ; and the
ground covered with climbing plants in rich
profusion, the wild convolvulus, honeysuckle,
helianthus, woodbine, and wild rose, giving it
the appearance of an overgrown, long-neglected
garden. Near the second rapid on the right
bank of the river is an extensive area of open

prairie-like ground, destitute of trees, but
covered with a dense growth of grasses and
climbing plants ; on it were two large mounds
of very peculiar appearance, looking like tumuli,
and called by the Indians "underground houses."
They were about 30 or 40 feet high and 100 feet
broad at the base. There were others also on the
left bank, but so hidden in the woods that their
size could not be ascertained. We could get no
information as to the origin or nature of these
tumuli, which looked not unlike mounds erected
over an ancient Indian battle-field.

At 6 P.M. we stopped for the evening meal,
and made preparations for drifting down the
river during the night, as is done by the Hudson's
Bay Company's boats. Just at sunset a most
extraordinary flight of insects appeared on the
river. They had pale, yellowish bodies about
¾-inch long, grey wings, and two long streamers
running out from the tail an inch or more in
length. They were moving up the river at a
great rate, in a solid column about ten feet high
and perhaps fifty feet broad, and at a distance
gave the appearance of a thick mist hanging
over the river ; nearer, they looked like a storm of
driving snow or sleet. As the gig pushed out

into the river amongst them, they parted in the
midst like a column of fours to let it go through,
carefully avoiding the boat.   They made a most
perceptible humming or buzzing noise, and, as
they touched the water, remained on it, apparently
unable to rise again.   The fish were rising all
round, devouring them greedily.

Having made our little preparations for the
night, all hands in the gig turned in except one
man to keep watch and steer; and as we lay in
the stern-sheets smoking a final pipe, we antici-
pated a pleasant drift down the river, and hoped
to get over a long way in this easy manner.   It
was a beautiful night, the moon was nearly at
the full, and the ripple of the water under the
bows of the gig, or the occasional stroke of
Ba'tiste's paddle had a most soothing effect.
But our hopes were doomed to be blighted; an
ominous bank of clouds to windward rose higher
and higher, a pelting storm of rain drenched us
to the skin, and a furious westerly wind, right in
our teeth, obliged us about midnight to put ashore.
One of the men rigged up the sail as a temporary
shelter, and we lay under it on the soaking wet
ground, trying in vain to get a little sleep.   The
ground was at a steep slope and unpleasantly

bumpy, and the welcome return of daylight found us cramped, cold, and wet, and glad to refresh ourselves with a cup of hot tea and resume our journey.

As we approached the mouth, the river became broader, the banks still very pretty, though with fewer open park-like bits ; long stretches of reedy, marshy ground fringed the banks, from which numerous young broods of ducks rose at our approach and flew past, presenting the most tempting double-shots. In the wide reaches of the river the strong westerly wind blowing against the current produced a rough chopping sea, against which we rowed hard for three hours, till we came to a small Hudson's Bay post, two miles from the mouth of the river, where we were glad to stop for breakfast. Just then a canoe came up, bringing letters from Rat Portage, announcing the arrival there of the six Hudson's Bay boats sent by the loyal English-speaking people of Red River. The letters begged Colonel Wolseley immediately to put two guns and as many regulars as possible into the boats and send them off to the settlement at once, as the people were in great dread of an Indian outbreak. The men who brought these letters were at once utilized as guides, and handed over to K Brigade, which came up at that moment.

The little post at which we breakfasted is kept by a half-breed named Morrison, and is called "Hungry Hall," from the fact of a former resident having been several times nearly starved to death. Morrison had a cow and a small patch of potatoes, and might have had a nice little farm had he chosen to take the trouble, for the alluvial soil on the bank of the river is very rich, and would well repay the labour of cultivation; but the half-breeds seldom care to till more ground than is sufficient to give them a scanty living. Leaving Hungry Hall, an extensive area of flat marshy land (portions of which would make good pasturage) marks the junction of Rainy River with Lake of the Woods. Our course here turning to the north, we made a fair wind of it, and setting both sails the gig slipped along, six or seven miles an hour, through the smooth water, protected by a number of long, low, sandy islands, on the other side of which the surf was beating angrily. Coming out from the shelter of these, we felt the full force of the gale, and soon shipped a green sea, which half filled the boat, and admonished us that it would be dangerous

M

to cross the open lake, so we lowered the sails
and rowed in to the nearest island. Captain
Macdonald's company of the 1st Ontario Rifles
coming up behind, followed our example; and
as the wind continued all that day (the 11th),
tents were pitched on the island to wait till the
gale moderated.

Lake of the Woods is an enormous sheet of
water about seventy-two miles long and nearly
as much broad, but divided by a large promontory
into three distinct lakes. On the south-western
coast are numerous long, low sand-hills, and
others in process of formation, which form a bar
of many miles in length, guarding the mouth of
the river. This part of the lake is sometimes
called Sand-hill Lake from these curious sand
dunes. The most noticeable feature of Lake of
the Woods is the peculiar green colour of the
water, arising from a profuse vegetable growth
(*confervœ*). These are a minute, tubular, needle-
shaped organism, about half an inch in length,
sometimes detached and sometimes clustered together in star-shaped forms: they abound all over
the lake, in some places so thickly that the water
has the consistence and colour of pea-soup. Some
of the deep bays receding from the lake, such

as Clearwater Bay, &c., are free from this growth, but it extends even a few miles down the Winnipeg River below Rat Portage. It was impossible to drink the water, or use it for making tea or cooking, until it had been carefully strained. The temperature of the lake, perhaps owing to these *confervæ*, was very high, 75° Fahr., yet it freezes over its whole extent every winter.

From the north-west corner of the lake, the distance across country to Fort Garry is only a hundred and fifteen miles, for about eighty of which, a road, passable for carts, had been already made. The remaining thirty-five miles pass through a continuation of swamps or "muskegs," and it was through these that some people were anxious that the troops should march, declaring it was quite feasible. Colonel Wolseley was very anxious to do so, as he would thereby have saved upwards of a hundred and fifty miles, besides avoiding the dangerous rapids of the Winnipeg River; but the information concerning this road was not sufficiently reliable, and he wisely declined to risk the experiment. The troops had therefore to cross the whole length of Lake of the Woods to its northern shores, where it empties its waters into Lake Winnipeg, by the magnificent

M 2

Winnipeg River. The southern portion of Lake of
the Woods is tolerably free from islands, and a
long stretch of open water lay before us as we
stood on "Detention Island," chafing at the delay
caused by the gale. To the westward not a sign
of land broke the vast expanse of water, stretching
away to the horizon, as if it had been the ocean
itself instead of an inland lake in the centre of a
continent; to the northward, a "traverse" of ten
miles to the nearest island lay before us, with the
"white horses" rearing their angry heads and for-
bidding all hope of a speedy release from our
little prison.

For the whole of that day and the next
the gale continued, and we were at our wits'
end to pass the time. The Colonel retired to his
tent and played "patience," but our only amusement was to go to the windward side of the
island, and watch the heavy line of breakers rolling
in on the sandy beach, and then contrast our
situation with that of friends at home grouse-shooting
on the moors. As a slight relief to the monotony,
the keen eye of Baptiste discovered something that
looked like a flag on an island to the east, and
by the aid of a telescope it was made out to be
the Union Jack, and two men were seen walking

on the shore close by. A canoe was sent over
to find out the meaning of this extraordinary
apparition, but returned reporting that they could
see nobody; the flag and the men were gone.
Whilst occupied with conjectures as to the explanation of this phenomenon, imagine our delight
when a canoe arrived from Fort Frances bringing
letters and newspapers from England! It was a
regular God-send, and many were the speculations
on the war just declared between France and
Prussia. But we could not even bet on the result,
for every one wanted to back the same side—
France. Short-sighted mortals! It was certainly
tantalizing to be wind-bound on a little island in
a lake far away in the centre of the vast North
American wilderness, cut off from all communication
with the outside world, whilst events of such tran-
scendent importance were taking place in Europe.
The situation was novel if not exciting. Robinson
Crusoe on his desert island was, however, worse
off than we were, for at all events we had plenty
to eat, though it was but salt pork and biscuit.

Towards the afternoon of the second day the
wind gradually subsided, and by sunset the water
was smooth enough to enable the large boats to
continue their route, and K Brigade re-embarked

and started off at 8 P.M. But there was still a heavy swell, and the Indians refused to budge a step, declaring it was not safe for the canoe, which would break in two pieces over the long waves. Colonel Wolseley, being determined to get on himself somehow or other, changed places with D——, and the gig was launched and prepared for a start. Just then, the flag we had seen on the island was explained by the arrival of three large Hudson's Bay boats, which proved to be some of those sent from Red River; they brought letters from Rat Portage, from Colonel Feilden, who reported that he had taken the other three himself and had started down the Winnipeg.

Now more than ever anxious to get on and catch the leading brigades, Colonel Wolseley resolved to start at once, and accordingly at 10 P.M. we put off. It was a bright, cloudless night with a full moon, and the men with light hearts and strong hands pulled with a will, glad to get away from their island prison. To the west and north no land was to be seen, to the east we could just make out the dim outline of a belt of islands several miles away, and behind us the island we had left was soon lost to view. We steered by the stars, shaping our course by the pointers of the

Great Bear. Although the wind had gone down there was still a heavy sea, a long rolling swell from the N.W., which justified the refusal of the cautious Iroquois to venture out in their frail birch-bark canoe. After three hours' hard rowing we came to an island where we put ashore at 1 A.M., made a big fire, and bivouacked till daylight. To me it had been a novel and curious sensation, which I enjoyed immensely; steering a boat at night by the stars, out of sight of land on a fresh-water lake, is not possible *everywhere.*

After four hours' rest, the crew of the gig were again under weigh at 5 A.M., steering N.N.W. A group of islands lay to the eastward, through which an opening was sought in vain to escape the rough sea, which was gradually but slowly subsiding; to the west, still no land to be seen, nothing to break the monotony of sea and sky. At last we got into an interminable labyrinth of islands, to find the right way through which would have required the education of a lifetime. On and on we went from "morn till dewy eve," steering by compass, with the aid of Mr. Dawson's map, a very inaccurate chart, until it was too dark to see any more, when we bivouacked on the nearest island.

Knowing that we could not be far from the

entrance to the river, we were off again next morning at 4 o'clock, hoping to reach Rat Portage by breakfast time. After rowing and sailing for some time we got into a deep bay, which proved to be a *cul de sac*, so we had to turn back again. From the course we had steered we knew we had reached the north shore of Lake of the Woods, but the entrance to the river we could *not* find. After trying a few more likely-looking openings to the northward in vain, the uncomfortable feeling began to creep over us that we had lost our way; however, there was nothing for it but to persevere, so on and on we blundered, hopelessly exploring every channel amongst the labyrinth of islands which appeared to lead in the right direction. We wandered on in this disagreeable way for hour after hour, until the sun began to get low in the sky, and we were still as far off the river as ever. This portion of Lake of the Woods is a mass of islands; in Lac des Milles Lacs and in Rainy Lake we thought we had seen a *few* islands, but anything to compare with the myriads in Lake of the Woods we had never before met with. We might have been wandering about amongst them to this day, had we not fortunately caught sight of an Indian encampment. Quickly rowing up, we found a good-humoured old man and two hideous old squaws, besides the inevitable children and white mongrel dog, all gazing at us with open eyes. We could not speak the Chippewa language, and they could not speak English or French, so here was a dilemma: but by dint of signs we made them understand what we wanted. A present of tea and biscuit to the women and a stick of tobacco to the man sharpened their intellects, and the man got into his canoe and paddled away, and we followed, devoutly hoping that he was taking us to Rat Portage. Such proved to be the case, and at 8 P.M., tired and hungry, we arrived at the portage, glad to get some supper (for we had fasted all day) and go to sleep. Our non-arrival had caused some fears for our safety, and Lieutenant Butler had started in a canoe to go and light a huge beacon-fire at the "Devil's Rock," a conspicuous, rocky island some fourteen miles out in the lake. We found that the Hudson's Bay boats and the canoe had arrived early that morning, having passed us on the lake whilst we were wandering about. The moral of my story is—Do not attempt to cross Lake of the Woods without a guide!

CHAPTER X.

THE WINNIPEG RIVER.

"Illi robur et æs triplex
Circa pectus erat, qui fragilem truci
Commisit pelago ratem
Primus."

THE Hudson's Bay Company's post at Rat Portage is but a small affair, three log-houses roofed with bark and enclosed by a high wooden palisading. The Company maintain thirteen men at this post, but nine of them are employed at small outlying posts in the vicinity. Mr. Macpherson, the official in charge, was most civil and obliging. He is a Scotch half-breed, a quiet, gentlemanly, elderly man, who has received a good education at Montreal. He had been for thirteen years buried alive at this post! Is it not a most extraordinary thing, that men of any education can be found to stand a life like that, utterly cut off from the rest of mankind,

receiving news from the outside world only once
or twice a year, to all intents or purposes dead or
sleeping ?   Like Jairus's daughter, one might say
of a man living at one of these Hudson's Bay posts
for a series of years,

οὐκ ἀπέθανεν ἀλλὰ καθεύδει.

I ventured to question Mr. Macpherson on this subject, and he replied simply, that he had long since
ceased to feel anything of the kind ; he had his little
farm and his wife and family, and was quite happy
and contented.   It is curious how soon men get
accustomed to a wild and solitary life; one can understand a man who had committed some frightful crime
rushing off, stung with remorse, to bury himself in
the remotest corner of the globe, as Sir Walter
Scott describes in the "Pirate," but it is not so easy to
understand how young men who have not completed
their fifth lustre can thus shut themselves up far
from the busy world, with no companions but
Esquimaux or Chippewa Indians.   Not theirs the
missionary fervour of men zealous for their faith, or
even the all-absorbing thirst for gold, for the Company do not pay their servants highly, and preclude
them by the most rigid rules from entering into any
speculation on their own account.   Yet they seem

to like the life, and after a brief return to civilization are generally glad to get back to their solitary posts. Mr. Macpherson had a few acres of wheat, barley, and potatoes, some pigs and cows, and any number of mangy-looking pariah dogs. These dogs are of all sizes and colours, nasty-looking brutes, but very useful. They do all the winter work, galloping for miles over the frozen snow, dragging small sledges.

At this place there are three portages; that is to say, the river, which is here some three miles broad, finds its way down to the lower level below by three distinct waterfalls. The regular portage, which is three miles from the Hudson's Bay post and principally used for big boats, is 130 yards long; but the portage we passed over is close to the post, about 300 yards long, and very rough. The morning after our arrival we breakfasted with Mr. Macpherson, and heard a great deal about the dangers of the Winnipeg River; indeed we heard so many stories of hair-breadth escapes amid the dangerous rapids and whirlpools, that, like the boy who has been regaled on thrilling ghost stories until he is afraid to go to sleep at night, we were half frightened out of our wits at the dangers that lay before us. Colonel Wolseley made every effort to procure guides and skilled bow-men and steersmen for each brigade, and sent off Lieutenant Butler in a light canoe to Fort Alexander, at the mouth of the river, to collect men from that post, and send them up to Islington Mission, where the most dangerous part of the river begins. In the evening of that day Lieutenant-Colonel McNeill, V.C., and Mr. Jolly arrived and joined our camp. They had left Shebandowan on the 3rd of August, and had come through as fast as possible in a birch-bark canoe.

At 2 P.M. on Tuesday the 16th we started again, two canoes and the gig, a pleasant party of six, to make the descent of the river Winnipeg. This noble river issues from Lake of the Woods through several gaps in the northern rim of the lake, and flows through many tortuous and distinct channels for many miles of its course. Its windings are so abrupt and opposite, that its course is sometimes N.N.E. and at other places S.W. by S. It is very broad and deep, sometimes expanding into large lakes, full of rocky islands and bounded by precipitous cliffs of granite. During its course of 163 miles it descends 350 feet by a succession of magnificent cataracts. Some of its rapids and falls present the wildest and most picturesque scenery, displaying every variety of tumultuous cascades and foaming rapids, with treacherous whirlpools, whitened with foam, and huge swelling waves rising massive and green over dangerous hidden rocks. It is quite beyond my power to convey an idea of the majestic scenery of this noble river, but it is so deeply impressed on my mind, that anything previously seen in the way of river scenery seemed at once to fade into insignificance before the grandeur of the Winnipeg River. Among the most beautiful of many very beautiful falls, the "Slave Falls" and "Silver Falls" bear away the palm.

We made the journey from Rat Portage to Fort Alexander in four days and a half, but to do this we had to work from early dawn to late at night, only snatching a couple of hours' rest for breakfast and dinner, and sometimes putting off our mid-day meal altogether, and making supper do duty for both. On the first evening, the 16th, we ran "Les Dalles" Rapids without any trouble, and camped about 25 miles from Rat Portage. The fine weather which had accompanied us from Shebandowan, here began to desert us, and drizzling rain with raw, cold, foggy weather took its place.

On the 17th, we ran the "Grande Décharge" Rapids, the first of any importance. The river, at least that portion of it which we followed (for there are numerous channels), is compressed at this point into a narrow cleft between high granite rocks, which force it down a steep incline with tremendous fury. Everything had to be taken out of the boats and carried over the portage, and then the boats were run down the rapids, four men rowing and the two Indians steering,—one at the bow, the other at the stern. Whilst at Rat Portage, Baptiste had cut and fashioned a fine broad paddle for this purpose out of a young spruce tree, and took his place at the bow flourishing this paddle over his head ready for action. We went over at a tremendous pace, so close to the cliff at one side (in order to avoid a half-sunken rock) that the starboard oars had to be unshipped and run in to avoid the cliff. Scarcely realizing the speed at which we were going, I was late in running in my oar, and consequently lost a rowlock by it, besides nearly breaking the oar and upsetting the boat. Of course when the oar touched the cliff it partially turned the boat's head, and Baptiste had to give a superhuman heave with his paddle to clear the sunken rock. In doing this his paddle broke in two like a stick of sealing-wax, and had he not, quick as lightning, seized a scull, which was fortunately at hand, and forced the boat's head round with it, we should have been on the rock and upset in the twinkling of an eye. It was a close

shave, but we had closer shaves than that before
we got to the mouth of the Winnipeg !

The same day we passed Yellow Mud Portage,
Pine Portage, Cave Rapids, and one or two smaller
rapids, which were run without lightening the
boats. On this river there are some twenty-five
portages, and any number of rapids of various
degrees of danger, but to do justice to their mani-
fold beauties would require a far abler pen than
mine. As I write, the recollections of those magnificent rapids and cascades crowd thickly upon me,

> " And I would that my tongue could utter
> The thoughts that arise in me."

Running a rapid is one of the most exciting things
in the world; independently of the danger of being
upset and drowned (which last would be a tolerable
certainty in anything *like* a rapid), there is a charm
about the novelty of it, combined with the wild and
picturesque scenery, which is wonderfully fascinating.
The Iroquois Indians are famous fellows for this
work, and far superior to the Chippewas. The
latter run rapids very fairly, but would avoid them
if they could, whereas I verily believe that the
former actually *prefer* rapids to smooth water. It
was quite a sight to see young Baptiste taking the

gig down a rapid. His post was in the bow, the
post of honour, and a better man it would be hard
to find. We soon got unlimited confidence in him,
and would have run any rapid under his leader-
ship. The other Indian we had in the gig was an
old weather-beaten Iroquois, an uncle of Baptiste's,
a man of enormous size and strength. He usually
took the stern, giving up the post of honour in the
bow to the younger and more active man. Our
preparations for running a rapid were very simple:
a rowlock was shipped in the sternpost, and Michel
took his place there, and steered with the stiffest
and heaviest oar in the boat. The rudder was never
used, as it did not give sufficient power. Baptiste
placed himself in the bow with a scull in his hand,
which he used as a paddle, and a spare one close by
in case of accident, a precaution which twice saved
us from upsetting. In order to give room to the
steersmen we pulled only four oars, which were
usually taken by the four best oarsmen in the gig.
As the noise of the rapid first reached our ears,
young Baptiste's eyes would sparkle with delight,
and even the phlegmatic old Michel, who scarce
ever uttered a word from morning to night, would
brighten up and look quite pleased. As we neared
the rapid, old Michel would say, "Hut! hut!" in

N

quick, sharp tones, which meant "pull, pull!" and pull we did, like demons, as if we had been doing the last fifty yards in a neck-and-neck race at Henley. As we took the first plunge, young Baptiste would wave his paddle in the air with one wild yell of delight, and then, as if ashamed of his momentary weakness, would address himself to his task, and with consummate skill and strength, plunging his paddle now this side, now that, would guide us down amidst the seething caldron of waters that hissed and boiled around, threatening every moment to swallow up the little gig. Not a word was spoken after Baptiste's wild shout, except rapid directions in the Iroquois language between the two Indians, the oarsmen pulling as if for bare life. Such moments of wild excitement, brief as they are, are worth years of tame existence, and make one feel inclined to look with pity on those who have never experienced that thrilling sensation that stirs every fibre in the frame and makes the heart leap with the most intense excitement. Is there a single man in the Red River Expedition who will ever forget the glorious rapids of that noble Winnipeg River? A hot corner in a day's battue-shooting, or a quick thing with the Pytchley, are exciting enough in their way, but they lack that element of danger which lends such a zest to every sport, when the heart is young and the life-blood courses quickly through the veins.

Many a dangerous rapid did we run in this way, but there was one that I shall never forget the longest day I live : it scared us all, and was indeed enough to frighten the oldest voyageur. Coming on to it from above we could not see what we were rushing into, but followed the lead of the Colonel's canoe, and before we knew where we were, we were in the middle of it. Imagine an enormous volume of water hurled headlong down a steep incline of smooth, slippery rock against a cluster of massive boulders, over which it dashed madly with a roar like thunder, foaming along until it reached the level below, where its exhausted fury subsided into circling eddies, and deep treacherous whirlpools. Into this fearful abyss of waters we dashed, old Michel boldly steering straight down the centre of it; and as we tore down the incline at railroad speed with the green white-tipped waves curling their monstrous heads high over the gunwale of the boat, we held our very breath for awe, and for a second or two forgot to row, till the sharp admonition

N 2

of Michel aroused us from our stupor. By a great exertion of skill on the part of the two Indians the boat's head was turned sharply to the left, and caught the back-water of the eddy, in which we floated quietly and in safety, and gazed in utter bewilderment at the mighty rapid we had just run with no worse accident than a good ducking. We were all rather scared, but one of our crew, a Londoner, was fairly pale with terror —"His coward lips did from their colour fly"— and though his comrades chaffed him freely, and each one disclaimed any fear on *his* part, yet there was not one of us who would have cared to repeat the experiment. This rapid was at Island Portage, and the gig was almost the only boat that ran it, the others being taken over the portage. It was the most dangerous rapid that we ran; the slightest touch on one of those huge boulders, and the boat must have gone to pieces instantaneously, crushed like a cockle-shell, and the crew would have been beyond human aid, for the whirlpools and eddies at the foot of the rapid would have sucked down the strongest swimmer.

But if he who first committed his frail bark to the sea must have been clothed in triple shield of brass, what shall be said of the man who first

ventured out in a birch-bark canoe, that frailest
of frail crafts, or still more of him who ran the
first rapid in such a crazy concern ? The slightest
touch on a rock is sufficient to tear a hole in it,
and in rough weather on the large lakes there
is always a danger of its breaking its back over
a wave. Still, in experienced hands, a bark canoe
is safe enough, and from its lightness and porta-
bility is the proper craft for navigating the rivers
and lakes of North America. Our boats were
declared to be quite unfit for running rapids, and
some of them undoubtedly were, but, with extreme
care and a more than ordinary share of good luck,
the soldiers managed to get along in them, and
descended the Winnipeg River in safety, though
with several hair-breadth escapes.

On the 18th we passed " Chute à Jacquot," and
" Trois Pointes des Bois," necessitating four portages
round these various falls, each having its own
special beauty, but all embracing scenery of the
loveliest description, and in the evening reached
" Slave Falls," one of the most beautiful bits on the
river.   The canoe portage is round a jutting ledge
of rock just above the falls, and very dangerous to
approach, except for skilled boatmen well acquainted
with the place. Colonel Wolscley's canoe, which

was leading the way, seemed to disappear, as if it
were going to shoot the falls, then suddenly turned
sharp round to the right and shot into land, quite
close to the edge of the falls ; but the Indians in
Colonel McNeill's canoe, who were Chippewas,
were afraid to venture, and stopped higher up.
The gig of course did not go near it, but went to
the regular portage for big boats, some 500 yards
above.   Our camp that night was on a level rocky
plateau, almost overlooking the falls, and in the
midst of such scenery as it is impossible to attempt
to describe.   The charm of romance, too, was not
wanting, for there is an old Indian legend connected
with the spot, which tells how, many years ago,
two Sioux prisoners, that had been long kept in
slavery by their enemies, the Chippewas, were one
day put out of their misery, with a refinement of
cruelty peculiar to the North American Indian.
They were bound back to back, placed in a canoe,
and allowed to go over the falls, where they
were of course dashed to pieces.   Hence the name
of "Slave Falls."

Next day, the 19th, we passed "La Barrière"
Portage, the "Otter Rapids" and the dreaded
"Seven Portages."   These are about three miles
long, and are simply an unbroken series of rapids,

falls, whirlpools, and eddies, necessitating seven
distinct portages, some of the approaches to and
departures from which are very dangerous, and
require skilful management.   On the following
day, the 20th, we reached Fort Alexander about
8.30 P.M., having made 16 portages in the last two
days.   D—— and I were quite done up ; we had
worked hard to keep up with Colonel Wolseley's
light canoe, and had been wet through all day
and every day.   In running one of the last
rapids we had a very narrow escape of being
upset.   Michel let the boat graze a rock : instantly
she heeled over on to her side, my oar was whipped
out of my hand, and I myself thrown violently
on my back, and for a moment I thought it was
all up with us, but she had only grazed, and
the rush of water carried her past ; and as she
righted, Michel picked up my oar and handed it to
me, and we went on as if nothing had happened.
It was a rough, boisterous rapid with strong eddies
and whirlpools ; we were quite alone, the two
canoes having gone on ; and it was nearly dark ;
so had we been upset, we should have had small
chance of getting ashore.

Of the eight portages we made that day one was
1320 yards long, the others varying from 150 to

350 yards. The two portages at the "Silver Falls" are steep and rough, but the falls themselves are worthy of their name. They are, I should imagine, the most beautiful on this river, or indeed on any river. It is impossible to conceive anything to surpass them. The volume of water is very great, and the scenery magnificent and picturesque; but we were in such a hurry to get on that we had little time to admire their beauties. The lights of Fort Alexander, visible some distance up the river, stimulated us to renewed exertions in the prospect of food and rest, and at last we arrived there, late in the evening, tired, wet, cold, and hungry. "No more portages, thank God!" we exclaimed, as the boat grounded on the sandy beach and we answered the cheery hail of the men of the 60th, all of whom, with the Royal Artillery and Royal Engineers, had arrived before us.

Fort Alexander is prettily situated on the left bank of the Winnipeg River, about a couple of miles above its junction with Lake Winnipeg. It is a larger and more important post than Fort Frances, and has a more imposing appearance, standing on high ground forty or fifty feet above the river. From the top of a wooden tower thirty feet high, built in front of the post, an extensive view can be had of the surrounding country ; to the right, the broad river is visible for many miles winding amongst the thick pine woods ; to the left, the vast expanse of Lake Winnipeg spreading out like the ocean itself, as far as the eye can reach. The soil round the fort is very good, and the crops luxuriant.

Mr. Donald Smith, who was awaiting the arrival of Colonel Wolseley, kindly gave us supper, to which we did ample justice. Seldom have I enjoyed anything more thoroughly than the fresh bread and butter which he set before us, or the pipe of peace which followed it, to which the happy consciousness that the hateful portage-strap would cease to gall our foreheads for some time to come, lent an additional feeling of freedom and repose.

CHAPTER XI.

THE latest news from Red River was to the effect that Riel had called a meeting of the French half-breeds, which was attended by 600 men, and had endeavoured to organize an armed resistance to the entry of the troops, but that his adherents had refused to join him in this mad attempt, and declined to have anything more to do with him and his plans. It seemed therefore that no opposition was to be apprehended, and in view of the certainty of being warmly welcomed by the loyal section of the inhabitants, Colonel Wolseley resolved not to wait for the Militia, but to push on at once with the Regulars. When passing the two leading brigades of the 1st Ontario Rifles a day or two before on the river, Colonel Wolseley had promised to wait half a day for them at Fort Alexander;

but as they did not arrive, the bugles sounded
the "advance" at 3 P.M. on the 21st of August,
and the men embarked and set sail to a favouring
breeze. There were eight brigades, about fifty
boats ; and as the little fleet ran down the river
before wind and tide, the sight was novel and
interesting. One might almost have fancied at a
little distance that it was a Danish flotilla, led by
some Viking of old, making a descent on an
enemy's coasts.

Colonel Wolseley accompanied Mr. Donald Smith
in a big Hudson's Bay boat, whose large square
sail towered over the little lugs of the smaller
boats, and led the way steering well " out to sea "
to make a good offing. The fleet followed as fast
as oars and sails would take them, and bore up
for " Elk Island," twenty miles off, which they
reached at sunset, and camped for the night in
a lovely little bay. It seemed as if nature had
designed this island for the express purpose of
sheltering the boats. The wind was southerly and
the bay had a north aspect, looking out on to
the lake, whose waves rippled gently on a smooth
sandy beach, charming enough to have made the
fortune of a European watering-place. And who
shall say that this little island and its beautiful

bay may not at some future day become the
favourite summer resort of the wealthy inhabitants
of Red River, the Brighton of the Winnipeg
belles ? When emigration shall have covered the
fertile prairies of the North-west with a teeming
population, and towns and cities have sprung up
over the length and breadth of the land, Elk
Island may rival the attractions of Newport and
Saratoga.

But when we ran into the little bay and sprang
ashore on the sandy beach, Nature had reigned
sole mistress for countless ages, and the primeval
woods rang for the first time to the sound of the
white man's axe. The life and bustle imparted to
the quiet bay by the arrival of the troops enhanced
the wild beauty of the scene ; and the boats drawn
up on the beach, with their sails half furled, the
white tents dotted about amongst the trees, the
ruddy glow of the camp-fires lighting up the figures
of the men as they bent over the *frying-pans* or
peered into the *kettles* with anxious interest,—all
these made up a picture worthy of an artist's
pencil.

An early hour next morning beheld the flotilla
again under weigh steering across the south-eastern
portion of Lake Winnipeg to the mouths of the

Red River. Lake Winnipeg is half as large again
as Lake Ontario! It covers an area of 9,000 square
miles, and is 264 miles long by an average of
35 wide. Not a bad-sized pond! The southern
portion of the lake is very shallow, the depth of
water not exceeding two or three feet at a distance
of a couple of miles from shore, and it is remarkable for the same green confervoid growth as Lake
of the Woods; the temperature of the water, too,
is very high. The fleet had a quick and prosperous
run from Elk Island, entering the Red River about
12.30 P.M. Red River flows into Lake Winnipeg
by three mouths through an immense area of low
land, of about the same level as the lake, and
covered with rushes and willows, which the spring
freshets annually overflow. Land, properly so called,
is not met with till six or seven miles from the lake.
The passage up the river was slower than that
across the lake, the boats having to keep in two
lines in proper order, by brigades. Colonel Wolseley sent his canoe ahead, with Mr. Irvine and
Lieutenant Butler to keep a sharp look-out, and
himself led the fleet, followed by Colonel Feilden.
At nightfall the camp was pitched on the right
bank just below the Indian settlement, and about
eleven miles from the Lower or Stone Fort. A

grand visit of ceremony was paid to Colonel
Wolseley by the chief of the Swampy Indians,
"Henry Prince," accompanied by a number of his
warriors, all decked out in feathers and paint. The
same sort of thing took place as at other "durbars"
held at Fort Frances with the "noble Indian,"
much talk of loyalty to their "Great Mother" and
steady adherence to British rule. The interview
ended as usual by a substantial present of pork
and flour; which appeared to afford the "braves"
the most intense gratification.

The most curious thing was the utter ignorance
of every one as to events going on in the neigh-
bouring parishes. No one could give any information as to what was going on in Fort Garry,
and the Indians declared that they had no idea
that the expedition had left Lake of the Woods
until they saw the boats coming round the point
opposite their wigwams.

Colonel Wolseley took every precaution to prevent the news of our arrival from spreading, and
after dark dispatched a trusty messenger on horseback to the Stone Fort to fetch Mr. Flett, the
Hudson's Bay Company's official in charge of that
post. He arrived in the middle of the night, but
could give no information, except that Riel and

his men were still in possession of the fort and
busily employed in carting away their plunder
from the Hudson's Bay Company's stores, and
that Bishop Taché was daily expected to arrive
from Canada with an amnesty for Riel in his
pocket. He also said that opinions differed as to
whether we should meet with resistance, whether
Riel would bolt, or come out to meet us and *hand
over* the duties of his office, but that Riel meant
fighting if he could only get his men to back
him up.

We were under weigh again next morning at daylight, in a drizzling rain, and reached the Stone Fort
or "Lower Fort Garry," as it is sometimes called,
at 8 o'clock. Here the kindness of Mr. Donald
Smith had prepared a sumptuous breakfast for the
officers, to which the most ample justice was done.
Colonel Wolseley ordered the boats to be lightened
of all superfluous stores in order to reach Fort
Garry if possible before dark, and only four days'
provisions were taken on, the remainder being left
at the Stone Fort.

Captain Wallace's company was detached as an
advanced guard and flanking party on the left
bank of the river, with orders to keep about a
quarter of a mile in front of the boats and to

detain all persons on their way up the river, so as to prevent the news of our approach from being conveyed to Fort Garry. A number of horses and carts were procured, and the men of this company were mounted on them, to their great delight. They seemed to think it fine fun scouring over the country as " Mounted Rifles." One man, being asked if he could ride, said he did not know whether he could or not, as he had never tried, and immediately proceeded to mount from the wrong side. Two signalmen with flags were sent with the mounted company, and were very useful in communicating orders to and fro, from the Commander's boat to the advanced guard. Lieutenant Butler was sent up the right bank on horseback, to patrol along the road and communicate with the boats every now and then. By these precautions it was found, as the force advanced, that the actual appearance of the boats was the first intimation that the people had of the arrival of the expedition. The country on the left bank is tolerably well settled, clean white houses and neat farms abutting on the river ; but the right bank is more wooded and very sparsely settled, there being at some places intervals of miles without a house to be seen. Many of the settlers turned out and fired off guns as salutes when they saw the boats, but no other demonstrations were made. The two 7-pounder guns were mounted in the bows of the Royal Artillery boats, and everything was in readiness in case Riel should dispute the passage up the river. In this way, keeping up a constant communication with the flanking party on our right (which being mounted was able to cover a large extent of country), we advanced steadily but slowly, pulling up against the stream, until it was time to halt for the night.

The camp was pitched on the left bank, six miles by land from Fort Garry, the distance by water being eight or nine. Outlying picquets were thrown out on both sides of the river, and a chain of sentries posted round the camp. Captain Wallace's company established itself in a farm-house about 600 yards off, with an advanced party on the main road, so that all communication between Fort Garry and the settlements in rear of the force was cut off. It had been Colonel Wolseley's intention to march at a very early hour next morning upon the fort, but about 10 P.M. a violent gale of wind sprung up from the N.W., accompanied by torrents of rain, which continued without intermission all night, rendering the roads nearly impassable. The unfortunate picquets and sentries looked more like drowned rats than human beings, and the men were so done up with cold and wet, that Colonel Wolseley was obliged to change his plans and continue the advance in the boats. Breakfast put a little life into the men, though everything was so wet that it was difficult to get the fires lit, and at 6 A.M. the men re-embarked and rowed on up the river, the rain still falling in torrents. Spies had been sent into the town of Winnipeg during the night to find out the actual state of affairs, and brought back news that up to that evening the rebel flag still "waved" over Fort Garry; and though vague rumours were afloat of the force being somewhere in the river, yet these were discredited by Riel, who with a few of his adherents still kept possession of the fort: also that Bishop Taché had arrived that day under a salute of twenty-four guns.

At 8 A.M. on the 24th the troops disembarked at Point Douglas, two miles from the town of Winnipeg, and formed up in open column of companies. The flanking party had brought a few horses and carts, so that there was sufficient trans-

port ready for the ammunition, engineers' tools, and
hospital. The guns were limbered up behind a
couple of country carts, and a few wretched ponies
served to mount Colonel Wolseley and his staff.
Covered by Captain Wallace's company in skir-
mishing order, and with a company behind as
a rearguard, the force marched straight on the
village of Winnipeg, the roads being ankle deep
in thick black mud, and the rain still pouring
in torrents.

Passing round the flank of the village, the fort
appeared in sight about 700 yards off, across the
open prairie. A few stray inhabitants in the village
declared that Riel and his party still held possession of the fort and meant to fight. The gates
were shut, no flag was flying from the flag-staff,
and guns were visible, mounted in the bastions and
over the gateway that commanded the approach
from the village and the prairie over which the
troops were advancing. It certainly looked as if
our labours were not to be altogether in vain.
"Riel is going to fight!" ran along the line, and
the men quickened their pace and strode cheerily
forward, regardless of the mud and rain. M. Riel
rose in their estimation immensely. The gun over
the gateway was expected every moment to open

fire, but we got nearer and nearer and still no sign ; at last we could see that there were no men standing to the guns, and, unless it were a trap to get us close up before they opened fire, it was evident that there would be no fight after all. " By God ! he's bolted ! " was the cry. Colonel Wolseley sent forward some of his staff to see if the south gate were also shut ; they galloped all round the fort, and brought back word that the gate opening on to the bridge over the Assiniboine River was wide open, and men bolting away over the bridge. The troops then marched in by this gateway, and took possession of Fort Garry after a bloodless victory. The Union Jack was hoisted, a royal salute fired, and three cheers given for the Queen, which were caught up and heartily re-echoed by a few of the inhabitants who had followed the troops from the village. It was still raining in torrents, and the whole place was one sea of black, slimy mud ; the men were drenched to the skin, and had been so during the previous night. Officers and men were therefore temporarily housed inside the fort, instead of pitching tents on the soaking wet ground.

Inside the fort were found several field-guns, some of which were mounted in the bastions and over the gateway, a large quantity of ammunition, and a number of old-pattern muskets, many of which were loaded and capped, showing that the intention had been up to the last moment to resist the entry of the troops. It is evident that Riel would have fought it out had his men stuck to him: he is reported to have said that very morning, that "it was as well to be shot defending the fort, as to give it up and be hung afterwards." The house that he and his "Secretaries of State" had occupied was found in a state of great confusion; the breakfast things on the table not yet cleared away, documents of all kinds, and the private papers of the ex-President lying about, betokened a hasty retreat. It appeared that Riel had refused to credit the report of the approach of the troops, until he actually saw them marching round the village, and had then hurriedly galloped off about a quarter of an hour before their arrival, taking the road to Pembina accompanied by Lepine and O'Donoghue. These fellows had been living in great luxury; the "Government House" was comfortably furnished with Mr. McDougall's furniture, captured last November; but though living in unaccustomed magnificence, they had not been able to get over their natural habits, and had allowed everything to get into a state of dirt and disorder.

No arrests were made by the military, but many of the inhabitants came forward offering to capture Riel and his gang if authorized to do so. Some of them wanted to be allowed to take him, *dead or alive*, and in that case would simply have shot him down on the first opportunity, without any parleying at all; but Colonel Wolseley had not been invested with any civil authority, and therefore told them that they must first obtain a legal warrant from a magistrate on sworn information, and that Mr. Donald Smith would then provide the means for executing it. A warrant was subsequently obtained from a justice of the peace for the arrest of Riel, Lepine, and O'Donoghue, on a charge of murder, false imprisonment, and robbery; but being found to be informal, it was never executed. In fact, there were no constables, and no civil authority until the arrival of the Lieutenant-Governor Designate, Mr. Archibald, pending which Mr. Donald Smith, at the urgent request of Colonel Wolseley, assumed the duties of Governor temporarily.

There is little doubt but that Riel and his two friends might have been easily taken prisoners, had Colonel Wolseley desired to do so, but in his position he did not desire to trench on the civil authority, and refused to allow his soldiers to be turned into policemen or constables. The three ringleaders made their escape across the bridge over the river Assiniboine, and then crossing to the right bank of the Red River, galloped up the bank for some distance, when, finding, doubtless to their surprise, that they were not pursued, they halted to rest. Next morning they could not find their horses, which had either been stolen or had strayed over the prairie during the night, so they pursued their journey on foot. After a while they wanted to cross to the left bank of the river to take the regular road to Pembina, but were unable to find a boat. Collecting some logs of wood and rails from the fences, they extemporized a raft, which they lashed together, in default of rope, by their braces and neck-ties, and other portions of their attire, and at last succeeded in getting across. Riel, however, lost one of his boots in the passage, and had to continue his journey barefooted. They had nothing to eat except a few dried suckers (fish), procured from a farm-house; and in this sorry plight, footsore, hungry, and wet, the ex-President and his two confederates reached the United States' territory, a melancholy example of the mutability of human

affairs, and the ups and downs of fortune. Riel
seemed to feel acutely the change in his position,
and said to a man whom he met travelling to the
Settlement, "Tell them that he who ruled in Fort
Garry a few days ago is now a houseless wanderer,
with nothing to eat but two dried suckers." In
Pembina but little notice was taken of the "fallen
potentates" by their former friends, and they subsequently separated, Lepine and O'Donoghue remaining on the American side of the line, whilst Riel
went to his own home in the little village of St.
Joseph's, which is a small hamlet, about thirty
miles west of Pembina, and chiefly inhabited
by half-breeds : here he was allowed to remain
unmolested.

The object of the expedition having been accomplished, Colonel Wolseley began to make preparations
for housing the two battalions of Militia, which
were to remain in the Settlement, and for the
return of the regular troops to Canada. For this
purpose he sent Lieutenant-Colonel Bolton to inspect
the road to the N.W. angle of the Lake of the Woods,
to see whether it was possible to send the troops by
that route, and so avoid the excessive labour of
taking the boats up the Winnipeg River. Lieut.-
Colonel Bolton returned after a week's absence,

reporting that the last thirty-three miles had not yet been cut out, and that there were such heavy morasses and thick woods that only a small body of men could get through ; the idea of sending the whole of the men by that route was therefore abandoned.

By the 27th August the brigades of Militia began to arrive, and on the 29th the first detachment of Regulars started in the boats on their return to Canada *vid* the Winnipeg River. By the 3rd September the whole of the 60th, with the Royal Artillery and Royal Engineers, had left Fort Garry by boat after a very brief sojourn. Only one company of the 60th, Captain Buller's, was sent by Mr. Snow's road as an experiment. This officer, by dint of much energy and determination, succeeded in getting his men safely through the swamps. Everything had to be carried on pack-horses, which were very lightly laden to enable them to get over the soft spongy muskegs. The company of the 1st Ontario Rifles which had been left as a garrison at Fort Frances, met this company of the 60th at the N.W. angle, and there exchanged boats and pack-horses.

Previous to the departure of the Regulars, Colonel Wolseley issued the following order of the day, congratulating the troops on the successful issue of their labours :—

"To the Regular Troops of the Red River Expeditionary Force.

"I cannot permit Colonel Feilden and you to start upon your return journey to Canada without thanking you for having enabled me to carry out the Lieutenant-General's orders so successfully.

"You have endured excessive fatigue in the performance of a service that for its arduous nature can bear comparison with any previous military expedition. In coming here from Prince Arthur's Landing you have traversed a distance of upwards of 600 miles.

"Your labours began with those common at the outset of all campaigns,—namely, with road-making and the construction of defensive works ; then followed the arduous duty of taking the boats up a height of 800 feet, along fifty miles of river full of rapids, and where portages were numerous. From the time you left Shebandowan Lake until Fort Garry was reached, your labour at the oar has been incessant from daybreak to dark every day. Forty-seven portages were got over, entailing the unparalleled exertion of carrying the boats, guns, ammunition, stores, and provisions, over a total distance of upwards of seven miles. It may be said that the whole journey has been made through a wilderness, where, as there were no supplies of any sort whatever to be had, everything had to be taken with you in the boats.

"I have throughout viewed with pleasure the manner in which officers have vied with their men in carrying heavy loads. I feel proud of being in command of officers who so well know how to set a good example, and of men who evince such eagerness in following it.

"It has rained upon forty-five days out of the ninety-four that have passed by since we landed at Thunder Bay, and upon many occasions every man has been wet through for days together.

"There has not been the slightest murmur of discontent heard from any one.

"It may be confidently asserted that no force has ever had to endure more continuous labour, and it may be as truthfully said that no men on service have ever been better behaved, or more cheerful under the trials arising from exposure to inclement weather, excessive fatigue, and to the annoyance caused by flies.

"There has been a total absence of crime amongst you during your advance to Fort Garry, and I feel confident that your conduct during the return journey will be as creditable to you in every respect.

"The leaders of the banditti who recently oppressed Her Majesty's loyal subjects in the Red River Settlement having fled as you advanced on the fort, leaving their guns and a large quantity of their arms and ammunition behind them, the primary object of the expedition has been peaceably accomplished. Although you have not therefore had an opportunity of gaining glory, you can carry back with you into the daily routine of garrison life the conviction that you have done good service to the State, and have proved that no extent of intervening wilderness, no matter how great may be its difficulties, whether by land or water, can enable men to commit murder or to rebel against Her Majesty's authority with impunity.

" G. J. WOLSELEY, Colonel,

Commanding Red River Expedition.

" FORT GARRY, 28th *August*, 1870."

The above order requires no comment, and shows in what light the performances of the troops were regarded by their commander.

The two battalions of Militia destined for the garrison of the Red River Settlement, were quartered, one at Fort Garry, the other at the Stone Fort, and all arrangements for their accommodation were personally seen to in detail by Colonel Wolseley himself before his departure. The Lieutenant-Governor, Mr. Archibald, arrived, *viâ* the Winnipeg River, on the 2nd September, and was duly installed amidst general approbation on the 6th. Colonel Wolseley, having accomplished his work,

handed over the command of the garrison to
Lieutenant-Colonel S. P. Jarvis, of the 1st Ontario
Rifles, issuing a complimentary farewell order to the
Militia similar to that addressed to the regular
troops, and left Fort Garry on the morning of
the 10th September by the road to the N.W. angle
of Lake of the Woods, accompanied by Mr. Irvine.
Lieutenant-Colonel Bolton and a small party had
started two days before by the same road, and
Lieutenant-Colonel McNeill, V.C., had previously
taken his departure on board the little steamer
International, to return to Canada, *viâ* the United
States, so that in an incredibly short space of time,
seventeen days from the arrival of the force, everything had been quietly and peaceably arranged, the
Governor installed, the garrison settled down to
its winter quarters, and the Regulars dispatched
on their return journey to Canada.

It is not necessary to dwell upon the difficulties
encountered on the return ; the same number of
portages had to be got over, the same number of
miles to be traversed, the only difference being
that the rapids of the Winnipeg and Sturgeon
rivers had to be painfully and laboriously ascended
by poling and tracking, instead of being swiftly
run. The troops, however, had a less quantity of

stores to carry over the portages, and the guns,
ammunition, &c. had been left in Fort Garry;
besides, they were up to their work and had the
satisfaction of feeling that each mile they passed
brought them nearer to their rest. By the first
week in October they had all reached Prince
Arthur's Landing, and as fast as they arrived were
conveyed in the steamships *Chicora* and *Algoma*
to Collingwood, and thence by train to Toronto
and Montreal. I cannot conclude this chapter
better than by quoting the General Order' which
was subsequently issued to the troops by His
Royal Highness the Field-Marshal Commanding-
in-Chief :—

"I. The Expedition to the Red River having completed the service
on which it has been employed, His Royal Highness the Field-Marshal
Commanding-in-Chief desires to express to Lieutenant-General the
Honourable James Lindsay, who organized the Force, and to Colonel
Wolseley and the officers, non-commissioned officers, and men who
composed it, his entire satisfaction at the manner in which they have
performed the arduous duties which were entailed upon them by a
journey of above 600 miles through a country destitute of supplies,
and which necessitated the heavy labour of carrying boats, guns,
ammunition, stores, and provisions, over no less than forty-seven
'portages.'

"II. Seldom have troops been called upon to endure more continuous labour and fatigue, and never have officers and men behaved
better or worked more cheerfully during inclement weather and its
consequent hardships, and the successful result of the Expedition
shows the perfect discipline and spirit of all engaged in it.

"III. His Royal Highness, while thanking the Regular Troops for their exertions, wishes especially to place on record his full appreciation of the services rendered by the Militia of the Dominion of Canada, who were associated with them throughout these trying duties.

(Signed)   " R. AIREY,
Adjutant-General.

"HORSE GUARDS, *November* 1870."

CHAPTER XII.

OUR first impressions of the new province of Manitoba were not very favourable. Drenched with rain and up to the ankles in mud, it was scarcely to be expected that we should look with pleased eyes on the level country spread out before us, covered with water like a vast swamp. But a sojourn of a fortnight removed these unfavourable impressions.

Fort Garry, which is simply a post of the Hudson's Bay Company, is a collection of brick and wooden buildings surrounded by a wall about ten feet high. The original fort was built in 1840, and was then nearly square, 100 yards long by 85 wide, with a stone wall and circular stone bastions at the angles. About the year 1850, a second portion was added to it, of the same size as the original; but the stone wall was not carried all round, the new portion being enclosed by a high wooden palisading on a stone foundation. This and the original stone wall are loopholed for musketry, and a wooden banquette runs round it to enable the defenders to fire from the loopholes. The bastions are also pierced for guns. The place is capable of being successfully defended against attacks of Indians or any enemy not provided with artillery; but even our small 7-pounder mountain guns would soon have made a breach in the wooden palisading, and a few shells would have quickly set the buildings inside in a blaze. The fort is crowded with buildings, which are used as stores and offices of the Hudson's Bay Company. It stands at the angle formed by the junction of the Assiniboine and Red rivers, which have here a width of about 160 feet and 500 feet respectively, and fronts on to the left bank of the Assiniboine, from which it is about 70 yards distant. Over this river there is a floating bridge, while the Red River is crossed by a scow ferry boat. The site is very pretty and commands a beautiful view of the prairie on all sides. To the north, about 700 yards off, is the town of Winnipeg, a collection of about 100 houses built at all angles to each other without any regard to symmetry. There are a few "general stores," a fair hotel, a photographic establishment, and a newspaper press ; but of tradesmen and skilled mechanics there is a great dearth : all such would find a good opening in Winnipeg, especially tailors, bootmakers, blacksmiths, bricklayers, carpenters, &c. Prices of all goods are very high, for though there is no import duty, yet freights are high in consequence of the long distances separating the settlement from the nearest railway. At present, the line is only open for a short distance beyond St. Paul's in Minnesota, but is rapidly being prosecuted northwards ; a line from Duluth and the cities on the south shore of Lake Superior is also projected as far as Pembina, to which point it will be easy to run a line over the level prairie from Fort Garry, and thus bring the settlement into direct communication with the United States and Canada. At present, goods have to be carted from St. Paul's to Frog Point, where they are taken down the Red River by water during the summer months. The Hudson's Bay Company run a small steamer, called the *International*, a flat-bottomed propeller, drawing about two feet of water, but very long, too long for the sharp turns and twists of the Red River ; in the spring or when the water is high, she can ascend as far as " Fort Abercromby,"

P

seventy miles above Frog Point, and about 130 below St. Cloud.

But as long as the only communication to the North-West Territory is through American soil, such a fact must tend greatly to Americanize the people, and if Canada desires to maintain her hold on this distant province, it is *absolutely indispensable* that she should construct a railway entirely within her own boundaries and be independent of her powerful neighbour. Such a line would probably run from Ottawa through the Lake Nipegon district north of Lake Superior to Lake Winnipeg, and would form the first portion of the future Pacific line to British Columbia. The Canadian Government appears to be alive to the importance of this, and sent out surveying parties during last summer in the direction of Lake Nipegon to find the best line for a railway. When once constructed as far as the valley of Lake Winnipeg, its future extension over the level prairie land for 1,200 miles to Edmonton House, and across the Rocky Mountains to British Columbia, becomes a mere question of time.

The present idea of making the route followed by the Expeditionary Force the regular highway for emigration from Canada to Manitoba seems to be impracticable, for though Mr. Dawson proposes to lessen the number of portages by building dams between some of the lakes, and talks of placing small steamers on Rainy Lake and Lake of the Woods, yet even then, the time which would be occupied in the transit, the expense attending it, and the total absence of supplies along the whole line, would be fatal objections. I should be sorry to form one of a party of emigrants struggling over those portages and through that barren and inhospitable region with their wives and families! The Indian question would also have to be settled before any emigrants could pass through—and if something is not done next spring to settle their claims, they will undoubtedly oppose the passage of any such parties. For the present, therefore, all emigration must take place through the United States, a long and roundabout road, and an expensive one.

Another unfortunate circumstance tending to throw obstacles in the way of the settler, is the unhappy reservation in the Manitoba Bill (*vide* Appendix C) of so large an extent of land, 1,400,000 acres, for the purpose of extinguishing the claims of the families of half-breed residents. Until this reservation is actually portioned off, no emigrant can acquire a title to land, or can venture to settle himself on a plot of ground, lest he should be turned out of it

to make way for a half-breed claimant.   Mr. Archibald surely has a hard task before him to portion
out this land in such a way as to interfere as
little as possible with emigration, in which of course
lies the future hope of the country.   That he will
successfully do so, and that the country will eventually get the better of the toils that have been
thrown around its young limbs by the short-sighted
policy of Sir George Cartier, there is no doubt.
The improvident half-breed, averse to steady toil,
and devoted to a wild life of freedom on the plains,
will soon dispose of his reservation of land to some
canny Scotch or English settler. · It is probable
that a large portion of it will eventually fall into
the hands of the Roman Catholic Church, which will
thereby acquire in Manitoba, as it has already done
in Quebec and Montreal, an undue preponderance
of wealth and power.   But the natural fertility of
the soil and its advantages as an agricultural and
grazing country must sooner or later triumph over
the puny efforts of Bishop Taché and his party to
check its growth and preserve the predominance of
their nationality.   The tide of emigration pouring
in from Ontario, and I trust also from the British
Isles, will soon sweep away the landmarks he has
tried to raise, and leave the French element in a

hopeless minority. The efforts of that far-sighted prelate have been directed to building up in the north-west a thoroughly French province, which would counteract by its influence the growing pre-

MONSEIGNEUR TACHÉ, BISHOP OF ST. BONIFACE.

ponderance of Ontario, and preserve the " balance of power" in the Parliament of Canada. So far he has succeeded, and by the establishment of the French language on an equality with the English throughout the new province, as well as by this reservation of land, he has done much to retard the growth of the country. At one of his interviews with Colonel Wolseley he could not help expressing his real feelings on this subject. "Ah!" said he, "how happy we were here in 'notre chère Rivière Rouge,' a quiet, contented, primitive people, far from the world and its troubles." And such he would have wished it to remain. In a pamphlet on the North-West Territory, published at Montreal in 1868, he dwells forcibly on the long and rigorous winter and the inaccessible nature of the country, and draws by no means an inviting picture of what is in reality one of the finest fields for emigration in the world. It is perhaps scarcely to be wondered at, that he, in common with the Roman Catholic clergy, should have viewed with regret and dismay the coming change, which threatens to deprive him of much of his influence in the settlement, over which he had previously ruled as a king.

That the Roman Catholic Clergy were at the bottom of the insurrection, nay, that they were its prime instigators and promoters, can be proved beyond question. Two of them in particular, Fathers Lestanc and Richot, made themselves most conspicuous. At the time the *émeute* broke out, Bishop Taché was in Rome attending the Œcumenical Council, but he had left Père Lestanc as

his vicar during his absence. This man, a French-
man *pur sang*, is a man of great ability and determination. His personal appearance reminds one
unpleasantly of the pictures of the Spanish In-
quisitors, a stern, ascetic countenance, as of one
who, had he lived in the days of the Inquisition,
would have revelled in the horrors of the torture-
room, and smiled at the shrieks of an *auto-da-fé*.
His influence amongst the French half-breeds was
very great; it was he who pulled the strings of
the puppets, and directed the course of events
after the first overt acts of rebellion. I have been
told on good authority that he was actually present
at the murder of Scott, which he openly abetted,
and told the firing party that they were doing a
righteous action, and were perfectly justified in
obeying the orders they had received to shoot Scott.

Père Richot, on the other hand, is a great contrast to Lestanc. He is a big, blustering fanatic,
a man of no great individual ability, a mere tool
of Lestanc's, but a dangerous instrument in the
hands of such an unscrupulous spirit. He is the
Curé of St. Norbert, the parish where the first
meetings of the disaffected took place, many of
whom he lodged in his house whilst the barricade
thrown across the road to Pembina to prevent

Mr. McDougall's entry was being maintained.
Throughout the movement he was a warm adherent
of Riel, and was one of the three delegates sent
to Ottowa by the Provisional Government. This
man had the impertinence to call upon Colonel
Wolseley just before Mr. Archibald's arrival, and
it was perhaps in disgust at the very cool reception
he met with from that officer that he announced to
his congregation on the following Sunday from the
pulpit, that "as no Civil Government had yet been
established, they were perfectly at liberty to form
another Provisional Government, and would be
justified in doing so," and also declared that "the
militia had been sent there to upset their religion."

But though Monseigneur Taché was not present
at Red River when the rising actually took place,
and though he was telegraphed for and brought
back from Rome at the public expense, and earnestly
besought by a confiding Government to allay the
spirit of disaffection in the North-West, yet it is
difficult to believe, in the face of positive evidence
to the contrary, that he was not aware of everything that was going on; it is, I repeat, hard to
believe that men who, like the Roman Catholic
clergy, are under such strict discipline, should have
ventured openly to foment an insurrection of this

description contrary to their Bishop's wishes or
unknown to him. Is it likely that Père Lestanc,
the confidential friend of the Bishop, selected by
him as his vicar to manage the affairs of the diocese
during his absence, would have dared to take upon
himself such a grave responsibility? As it happens,
we have direct evidence in the Bishop's own hand-
writing, proving on what terms of familiarity he
was with Riel and O'Donoghue, and letters of his
are extant which speak of the cause they all had
at heart, and the support which their powerful
friend at Ottawa (Sir G. Cartier) would continue
to give them. Amongst the private papers of Riel,
left lying about in confusion in his room, three
letters from Bishop Taché to the President fell into
my hands, seriously compromising himself and Sir
George Cartier. The most important of these
letters was subsequently lost in a most mysterious
manner, before any copy had been taken of it, but
the others, as also one from Lestanc, are still in my
possession, and I give one of them *in extenso* as
a sample :—

" HAMILTON, 24e *Juillet*, 1870.

"M. Ls. RIEL, PRÉSIDENT.

"MONSIEUR LE PRÉSIDENT,

"J'ai eu une entrevue hier avec le Gouverneur Général à Niagara ; il m'a
dit que le Concil ne pourrait pas revenir sur la décision prise d'envoyer

Mr. Archibald par les Possessions Britanniques, et ce, pour des raisons, *très bonnes*, qu'il m'a expliquées et que je vous communiquerai plus tard. Nous ne pouvons donc pas arriver ensemble comme je l'avais espéré. Je ne serai pas seul, car j'aurai avec moi des gens qui viennent pour nous aider. Mr. Archibald regrette de ne pouvoir pas arriver par Pembina : il désire pourtant arriver au milieu *de nous*, et ce, avant les troupes ; c'est pourquoi il serait bien content s'il y avait moyen de lui trouver *un chemin* soit par la Pointe de Chênes soit par le Lac des Roseaux, aussi je vous prie de *faire faire* des recherches à cet égard, afin d'obtenir le résultat que nous nous étions proposé. *Il faut* qu'il arrive parmi et par nos gens. Je suis très content de ce Mr. Archibald, je crois vraiment que c'est l'homme qu'il nous faut ; déjà, il parait comprendre très bien la position et la condition de notre chère Rivière Rouge, et semble en aimer le peuple : ayons donc confiance que le bon Dieu nous a bien servi malgré notre indignité. *Soyez sans inquiétude ;* le temps et la confiance nous apporteront ce que nous désirons tous [1] et qu'il est pourtant comme impossible de mentionner vu l'excitation de certains esprits. . . . Les fureurs du mois d'Avril nous ont préparé les grâces du mois de Mai ; soyons persuadés que les petites rages du mois de Juillet preparent le triomphe du mois d'Août. Nous avons des amis sincères, devoués et puissants.[2] Je pense partir de Montréal le 8 du mois d'Août, en sorte qu'il est probable que j'arriverai vers le 22 du même mois. La lettre que j'ai apportée a été envoyée en Angleterre ainsi que *celles* que j'ai écrites moi-même et que je vous ai lues. Les gens de Toronto ont voulu faire une démonstration contre l'amnistie, et malgré le *puf* des journaux ils n'ont jamais osé donner le chiffre insignifiant des personnes presentes. Quelques individus ont voulu en parler ici à Hamilton, mais les journaux ont empêché cet effort de zèle que tous les gens sensés désapprouvent ouvertement. Je suis ici par hasard et retenu parceque c'est dimanche. Mes saluts à Mr. O.[3] et autres du Fort. Priez bien pour moi, je ne vous oublie pas.

" Votre pauvre Evêque et aussi je . . . .

" Votre meilleur ami,

" ALX. EV. DE ST. BONIFACE."

The italics are the Bishop's, and the tone of the letter speaks for itself, and ought to convince the

---

[1] That is to say, the much-desired amnesty.
[2] Sir G. E. Cartier (?).   [3] O'Donoghue (?).

most sceptical of the real connection between the Bishop and the "President." The attempt to induce Mr. Archibald to enter the settlement under his, Bishop Taché's, auspices was a bold effort to retain the reins of power in his own hands, and make the new Governor rule through the French party. Fortunately for the peace of the settlement, this plan failed.   Mr. Archibald made his entry by the Winnipeg River, alone, in his own canoe, although Bishop Taché had sent horses to meet him at the north-west angle of the Lake of the Woods ; and thus avoided giving offence to the loyal section of the people, as he undoubtedly would have done had he been introduced by the French party.

The population of the province of Manitoba, exclusive of Indians, may be roughly taken as about 15,000.   Of these the greater portion are half-breeds, whether descended from French, Scotch, English, or Irish parents.   The French half-breeds are by far the most numerous, and the French language, or a patois of it, is mostly spoken throughout the Territory.   The half-breed is *the* inhabitant of Red River ; he does the work of the country, and is to be seen everywhere, in the settlements, on the rivers, on the prairie—in fact, he is ubiquitous. According to the amount of European or Indian blood in their veins, the half-breeds differ from one another much in the same way as a quadroon in the south differs from a full-blooded negro. From the civilized half-breed farmer, who prides himself in copying the manners and customs of his white ancestors, and lives on his little estate in comfort and affluence, to the semi-savage half-breed hunter of the plains, but little, if at all superior to the full-blooded Indian, who scorns the restraints of civilization, and revels in the freedom of a wild life on the boundless prairie, the difference is very great, though both are included in the generic term " half-breed." This term, which grates rather unpleasantly on European ears, is not considered as by any means a term of reproach. The half-breed is proud of his mixed descent, in many cases prouder of his Indian blood than of its white admixture. An excellent horseman, a good shot, with an eye like a hawk, and the keen, unerring instinct of his mother's race, added to considerable muscular strength and a supple elastic frame capable of enduring severe and continuous fatigue, the half-breed is the great hunter and trapper of the prairies, the guide to whose semi-savage instincts the white man has to trust himself, and who seldom betrays confidence reposed in him. In the settlements he may be

seen loafing about the whiskey saloons, clad in a
long blue cloth capote with brass buttons, purchased from the company's stores ; but when
hunting on the plains he discards the capote in
favour of a leather shirt with deer-skin mocassins
and leggings, tastefully embroidered with many
coloured beads and porcupine quills. Though given
to the curse of strong drink when in the settlements, that curse of "whiskey" which seems to
overshadow the land and is rapidly exterminating
the aboriginal red-skin, yet when he is "en voyage,"
the half-breed will abstain for weeks and months
from the accursed "fire-water," only alas ! to break
out into frightful excesses when he gets back to
the temptations of the whiskey saloon. This trait
of character is happily illustrated in the "North-
West Passage by Land," in the description of "La
Ronde," the hunter who accompanied Lord Milton
and Dr. Cheadle in their journey across the Rocky
Mountains. He is a very favourable specimen of
the French half-breed, and lives in a pretty little
cottage about a mile from Fort Garry. When taxed
with his devotion to the bottle, he replied—"Je ne
bois pas souvent ; mais quand je bois, je bois—c'est
ma façon, voyez-vous ;" and he was right ; when they
drink they *do* drink with a will. In the town of

Winnipeg every other house seems to be a whiskey shop, and for the first two or three days after our arrival the place seemed turned into a very Pandemonium—Indians, half-breeds, and whites, in all stages of intoxication, fighting and quarrelling in the streets with drawn knives, and lying prostrate on the prairie in all directions, like the killed and wounded after a sharp skirmish. Fortunately, the stock of whiskey was limited, and was quickly consumed, so that these drunken orgies soon came to a natural end.

With the exception of the little village of Winnipeg, the farm-houses of the settlers are not built on the prairie, but follow the line of the rivers. From White Horse Plains, some sixty or seventy miles up the Assiniboine River, down to Fort Garry, thence along the banks of Red River to the Indian settlement, about eight or ten miles from Lake Winnipeg, and also up the Red River for a few miles *above* Fort Garry, these houses are dotted along the banks more or less thickly. No "locations" have as yet been taken up at a distance from the river, principally because there has been no necessity to do so, and men naturally preferred a river frontage if they could get it. The difficulty of getting water seems also to have operated against interior settlement : they *say*, that although water is found at a depth of thirty or forty feet, it is generally brackish ; but this difficulty will probably vanish when put to the test of experience.

The prairie roads are good. From Fort Garry to the Indian settlement thirty miles down the Red River, there is a good road over the prairie called "the King's road;" it runs nearly straight, not following the sinuosities of the river, but meeting it at some points, and at others being a mile or more from it. At such places there is an inner road along the bank of the river. I was much struck on one occasion when riding down to the Indian settlement with the comfortable well-to-do appearance of the people, and their neat houses and farms. The fences are made of poplar poles piled on each other between two uprights, not a bit like the zigzag "snake fences" of Canada ; and the houses are mostly frame-houses neatly white-washed. For the first twelve miles the road passes over the open prairie ; then the country gradually becomes wooded, with small clumps of poplar, sometimes fenced round like a young plantation in England. These little patches become thicker and more frequent, till at last the road becomes a single track through the wood, with open spots here and there, instead of, as before, a number of tracks side by side, equally good and open to the selection of the traveller. In this prairie country you can drive a horse and waggon anywhere: there are no fences to stop you, and no notices of "prosecution for trespass." There is an inexpressible charm in the freedom of the "boundless prairie"; you feel as if you could go anywhere; there is an exhilarating feeling in the pure bracing air, which seems to clear the brain, to lengthen the vision, and to free you from the trammels of ordinary existence. No wonder it has produced so fine and handsome a race of men as are the half-breeds. I passed several of them on the road, some mounted, some on foot. Each man had his long rifle over his shoulder and his powder-horn by his side, just like the warlike Rajpoots of Central India, upright, fine-looking fellows, with a certain air of freedom and nobility about them, looking you straight in the face, and touching their caps or nodding in token of respect or salutation.

What a future must surely be in store for this magnificent country, destined to be the granary of the Old World, and the birthplace of millions of free men! Gazing on the fertile prairie spread out before the eye, smooth and level as a billiard table, and stretching away to the west, to the west, for hundreds of miles, lacking nothing but the toil of the husbandman to convert it into fields rich with yellow waving corn, one can fancy the future inhabitant of the soil looking proudly out on his rich inheritance, and exclaiming, with a slight adaptation of Byron's well-known lines—

> " O'er the rich acres of our vast prairie,
> Our hopes as boundless and our souls as free,
> Far as the heart can wish, the fancy roam,
> Survey our empire and behold our home."

At present the cultivation of the soil is carried on in a primitive fashion. Each settler owns about fifteen or twenty head of cattle, which he turns out to feed in the open prairie : hay for the winter is cut anywhere, provided it be upwards of two miles from the river, that distance having been reserved by a local law. Grass of the most excellent quality is to be had for the cutting; milk, butter, and eggs are abundant and good ; and the soil is so rich that very little farming is required to produce a fine crop. The farmer takes but little trouble with his fields, never puts manure on them, and, having no market for his surplus produce, only cultivates enough land to feed himself and his family. But as the country becomes more populous

Q

and towns and villages spring up, the people will
acquire a market of their own ; and when the
connection with Canada and the United States by
railroads is fully developed, they should be able
to compete successfully in the markets of the world.
The opening up of those fertile regions ought to
give a great impetus to emigration, as it will enable
the emigrant from the British Isles to retain his
allegiance to the old flag, whilst working out for
himself a competence in the far West by honest
toil. The chief obstacle to emigration to Canada
from England has been the fact of the country
being covered with a dense forest, requiring great
labour at the outset to clear a plot for cultivation,
and labour of the severest kind, to which the immi-
grant is probably but little accustomed. But in
Manitoba there is no such difficulty. There is the
land, as fertile as any in the world, and much more
so than in many parts of Canada, ready waiting
for the plough. The husbandman has nothing to
do but commence his ploughing and sowing at once.
Every inducement to emigrants, and every help to
reach the country, will no doubt be freely given
by the Canadian Government, and the tide of
emigration now flowing so largely to the United
States, and annually converting thousands of British

subjects into citizens of a State with which England *may* be at war to-morrow, will be turned into a new channel, to irrigate the fertile prairies of the North-West with a living stream of happy and contented people, and to make of United Canada a powerful and prosperous nation. May this dream be realized! Should one single intending emigrant be induced by these words of mine to select Mani-toba for his future home, then *I* shall not have written in vain, and *he* will never regret it.

But, as I would not wish to draw a picture of unsullied brightness, or intentionally deceive the reader into the belief that everything is "couleur de rose," I must put in the dark shadows as well and not forget to mention the "grasshoppers" which occasionally visit the settlement, and, like the locusts in the land of Egypt, "eat every herb of the land, and all the fruit of the trees." These grasshoppers are about an inch long, of a greenish yellow colour. They come about the middle of July or beginning of August. Their flight is from south-west to north-east, in dense clouds, "so that the land is darkened" with them. Wherever they alight they make a desert, eating up every blade of corn and grass, and stripping the trees of their leaves. Two or three days after their arrival, the female lays her eggs, which she does by digging a small hole in the ground, in which she immerses about half her body. The eggs are covered with a kind of waterproof bag, which preserves them until the following spring: then, about the first week in May (no matter how severe or how long may have been the winter's frost), the young grubs make their appearance, and do as much or more harm than the grasshoppers themselves, eating up every green thing in the fields and gardens. Each insect will lay about five hundred eggs.

In the summer of 1868, the grasshoppers came in such countless myriads that they were lying piled up against the angles of the bastions and walls of Fort Garry to a depth of three feet. The stench from their dead bodies was almost insupportable, and they had to be *carted* away and thrown into the river. Nothing will arrest their flight or turn it off in another direction. Huge bonfires and columns of dense smoke have been tried in vain, and the unhappy farmer can do nothing but resign himself to his fate, and behold with what philosophy he may the destruction of his crops. Happily, this dreadful plague seems to recur less frequently than in former years, and with less severity. Last year, 1870, the grasshoppers came

very late in the season, and did only partial harm
in the upper parts of the settlement, so that this
year crops may be sown without so much fear.   It
is a curious fact, which I have never heard explained,
that as the waste lands become reclaimed and cul-
tivated the visits of the grasshoppers gradually
cease.   In Minnesota, they are not nearly so bad
as they were a few years ago, and in Illinois and
Iowa, which were formerly subject to their ravages,
they are now almost unknown.   It is therefore fair
to hope that as the North-West Territory is brought
more and more under cultivation, and becomes
more settled, this terrible plague will disappear
altogether.

The thick woods and swamps which fringe the
western margin of Lake of the Woods, terminate
very abruptly about thirty miles east of Fort Garry,
and the open prairie country commences in a very
clearly-defined line, and stretches away to the westward, with scarce any intermission for 1,200 miles,
right up to the Rocky Mountains.   Much of this is
unfit for cultivation, but a large proportion, called
"The Fertile Belt," and comprising many millions
of acres, consists of as rich and fertile land as is to
be found anywhere in the world.   Herds of moose
and cariboo inhabit the woods east of Fort Garry,

and in the open country prairie-chicken are abundant. It seems surprising that these birds should be
able to stand the severe and long-continued winter,
which is of about the same duration as that of Lower
Canada ; but as the depth of snow rarely exceeds two
feet, they are enabled to feed on the red berries or
seeds of the wild rose, which grows in great luxuriance all over the prairie, and is seldom entirely
hidden by the snow.

Buffalo are no longer found nearer than 300 miles
west of Fort Garry, and are gradually being driven
further and further west by the advancing stream of
white civilization ; so that the day is, I fear, not far
distant when these noble animals, like the deino-
therium and mastodon of former epochs, will become
extinct, or only known to future generations by a
few specimens that may survive in our zoological
collections. For a couple of months' shooting trip in
the fall of the year, Fort Garry would make a good
starting-point ; guides and hunters, and other necessaries for a prairie life could be procured there.   A
large spring waggon, drawn by two horses, would
be large enough for a party of four (including two
guides), and would contain all their impedimenta,
which ought to consist simply of blankets, a change
of clothes, and lots of ammunition.   Very little pro-

visions would need to be taken, only some flour and
groceries, and a little pemmican.   The shot gun
would supply ample food in the shape of prairie-
chicken and wild fowl of all descriptions, until the
buffalo country was reached.   Two spare horses
should certainly be taken for running the buffalo.
The whole party might sleep in the waggon during
wet weather, under a white canvas covering,
stretched over the waggon on hoops, as is done
by parties of emigrants ; or, better still, if a light
tent were taken, made of grass-cloth, weighing only
twenty pounds, and large enough to accommodate
four men, it would render the sportsmen more independent.   For battery, I should recommend a
double-barrelled shot gun for small game, and for
the buffalo one of Westley Richards' breech-loading
carbines, very similar to the Martini pattern, and
the hardest-hitting and quickest-loading weapon
yet invented, as I can testify from personal experience.   I can scarcely fancy anything more
enjoyable than a trip such as I have briefly
sketched.

About twenty miles below Fort Garry is another
post of the Hudson's Bay Company, called " Lower
Fort Garry," or the " Stone Fort."   It is a large
oblong affair, surrounded by a high stone wall, with

round towers or bastions at the angles, and is a place
of some strength. It stands on the left bank of the
river, which is here about eighty yards wide, and
flows between high precipitous banks. During the
recent disturbances, the residents in the neighbourhood, being principally of English descent, were loyal
to the British Crown, and Riel dared not show himself amongst them. Colonel Dennis held possession of
the Stone Fort for some time, with a garrison of fifty
of the loyal Indians from the Indian village, ten
miles further down the river. These Indians belong
to the tribe of Saulteux or Swampies, and are generally called "The Swampy Indians." They have
been converted to Christianity, and profess the
Protestant faith, though speaking no language but
their own, the Chippewa. Their pastor is the
Reverend Mr. Cochrane, one of themselves, a full-
blooded Indian, but a most intelligent, well-read
man. His pretty little church, and neat white
parsonage-house and school adjoining, stand on
the right bank, at a bend of the river, and are
almost the first buildings that catch the eye when
ascending the river, and form a pleasing contrast
after the wild and ever-changing scenery of the Winnipeg River. The Swampies and their chief, Henry
Prince, remained thoroughly loyal during the dis-

turbances, and refused to have anything to do with
Riel, although their loyalty was severely tried by
the machinations of Riel's Indian agent, a man
named James McKay, who was sent down to
seduce them from their allegiance. This James
McKay was a man of the most elastic political
faith, and, after working for Riel, and trying to
embroil the country in the horrors of an Indian
war, he turned very loyal *on the approach of the
troops*, and like other renegades received his re-
compense by being taken into Government pay,
and employed to make the road to the north-west
angle of Lake of the Woods. This mode of reward-
ing rebellion has several high precedents in Canada
to recommend it, and, indeed, is not unknown in
other countries, much on the same principle on
which an incorrigible poacher is frequently converted into a good gamekeeper. Verily, they have
their reward !

The Red River Settlement boasts of a Protestant
as well as a Roman Catholic Bishopric. The latter
has its head-quarters in the parish of St. Boniface,
just opposite Fort Garry, on the other side of the
river, where a cathedral, a school, and a nunnery
alongside the Bishop's palace present quite an imposing appearance. The Protestant cathedral or

church is a few miles down the river, and the
diocese is under the charge of Bishop Macrae, to
whose good sense and prudent counsels the people
of Red River owe a debt of gratitude, as he was
mainly instrumental in preventing the outbreak of
civil strife and in smoothing down the animosities
of race and religion. To him, and also more especially to the Rev. Mr. Gardiner, the Presbyterian
clergyman, the successful descent of the Winnipeg
River by the boats of the Expedition is greatly due ;
for, as has been mentioned in a previous chapter,
it was through their exertions that six large
Hudson's Bay boats and a number of skilled boatmen, acquainted with the rapids of the Winnipeg
River, were despatched to Rat Portage and aided
materially in bringing the troops down without
accident. To defray the expenses of this undertaking, Bishop Macrae, Archdeacon McLean, and
Mr. Gardiner contributed liberally from their private
funds, the last-named gentleman himself accompanying the little expedition. Honour to whom
honour! Let not their patriotism and energy be
forgotten by the people of Winnipeg.

The new Governor of Manitoba, the Honourable
A. G. Archibald, is a native of Nova Scotia, where
he filled several high offices previous to the con-

federation of the British North American Provinces in 1867. Being a Confederate, he lost his seat during the violent storm raised against the Union by the Antis, but was subsequently re-elected when the agitation began to subside. Personally he is a fine, handsome, benevolent-looking man of forty-five or fifty, a clever lawyer, and agreeable, gentlemanly, and well read. The liberal and enlightened policy which he has inaugurated, bodes well for the future of the great country committed to his care. He showed his appreciation of the work done by the Expedition, by writing a highly-complimentary letter to Colonel Wolseley from the Indian Settlement, before even he had reached Fort Garry. As this letter is not long, I must be excused for quoting it in full :—

"INDIAN MISSION, RED RIVER,
Sept. 2nd, 1870.

"DEAR COLONEL WOLSELEY,

"I take the earliest opportunity in my power to congratulate you on the magnificent success of the Expedition under your command. I can judge of the work you have had to do all the better from having seen for myself the physical obstacles that had to be met and overcome ; obstacles which, I assure you, exceeded anything I could have imagined. It is impossible not to feel that the men who have so triumphed over such difficulties must not only have themselves worked well, but also must have been well led, and I should not be doing justice to my own feelings if I were not, on my arrival here, to repeat the expressions of admiration extorted from me as I passed along, in view of the difficulties you had to meet, and which you have so triumphantly surmounted.

"I have the honour to be, dear Colonel Wolseley,

" Yours very truly,

" A. G. ARCHIBALD.

" To Colonel Wolseley, Fort Garry."

This letter gave great pleasure to the officers and men of the Expedition, and doubly so, on the principle that "bis dat qui cito dat!"—a principle too frequently lost sight of in the bestowal of praise, though not in that of censure.

In bringing this short narrative to a close, it may not be amiss to compare this Expedition, in its political bearings and results, with other Expeditions, and notably with the recent Abyssinian Expedition. The latter was undertaken for the purpose of rescuing some half-dozen English subjects from the hands of a barbarian chieftain; it was supported by the sentiment of the whole English nation; it was magnificently and successfully carried out under the direction of Sir Robert Napier, and, happening at a time when no foreign war or event of importance distracted the attention of England, it commanded the sympathy, and by its success flattered the vanity, of all classes of Englishmen. But at what a cost! £9,000,000 is surely a heavy price to pay for a brilliant and successful, but by no means, in its results, an important undertaking.

The Red River Expedition, while it had to be conducted over a greater distance, and through a more inhospitable region as well as greater physical obstacles, was overshadowed in its very infancy by the great European war, which entirely . absorbed all the interest and sympathy of the public ; this no doubt accounts for much of the general indifference felt about the whole affair. It is not, however, too much to say that, in its political bearings and results, no event of similar importance has for many years been accomplished with so little expenditure of time and money. From first to last the time occupied was five months, the expenditure about £400,000, of which England only pays one-fourth. Under the energetic and skilful conduct of Colonel (now Sir Garnet) Wolseley, no accident or mistake occurred throughout the whole Expedition, and not one single life was lost !

When the excitement of the present great war on the Continent has subsided, and the bloody battles and sieges which have gone far to ruin one great nation, and have caused untold misery to thousands of French and Germans, have become matter of history, then may the less dazzling but bloodless campaign of the Red River Expedition claim its share of public attention—a campaign which can tell no tale of sickening horrors or devastated homes, but in its peaceful accomplishment has carried and asserted the power of Great Britain to the Far West, and while opening up a virgin soil for her sons in a distant land, has added yet another province to that Empire on which the sun never sets.

APPENDICES.

APPENDIX A.

LIST OF RIGHTS.

1. THAT in view of the present exceptional duties of the North-West, duties upon goods imported into this country shall continue as at present (except in the case of spirituous liquors) for three years, and for such further time as may elapse until there be uninterrupted railroad communication between Red River Settlement and St. Paul, and also steam communication between Red River Settlement and Lake Superior.

2. As long as this country remains a Territory in the Dominion of Canada, there shall be no direct taxation, except such as may be imposed by the Local Legislature for municipal or other local purposes.

3. During the time this country remains a Territory in the Dominion of Canada, all military, civil, and other public expenses in connection with the general government of the country, or that have hitherto been borne by the public funds of the Settlement, beyond the receipt of the above-mentioned duties, shall be met by the Dominion of Canada.

4. That while the burden of public expense in this

R

country is borne by Canada, the country be governed under a Lieutenant-Governor from Canada, and a Legislature, three members of which, being heads of departments of the Government, shall be nominated by the Governor-General of Canada.

5. That after the expiration of this exceptional period, the country shall be governed, as regards its local affairs, as the provinces of Ontario and Quebec are now governed, by a Legislature elected by the people, and a Ministry responsible to it, under a Lieutenant-Governor appointed by the Governor-General of Canada.

6. That there shall be no interference by the Dominion Parliament in the local affairs of this Territory other than is allowed in any of the provinces of the Confederation ; and that this Territory shall have and enjoy, in all respects, the same privileges, advantages, and aids in meeting the public expenses of this Territory as the Confederated provinces have and enjoy.

7. That while the North-West remains a Territory, the Legislature has a right to pass all laws local to the Territory, over the veto of the Lieutenant-Governor, by a two-third vote.

8. A Homestead and Pre-emption Law.

9. That while the North-West remains a Territory, the sum of 25,000 dols. (twenty-five thousand dollars) a year be appropriated for schools, roads, and bridges.

10. That all public buildings be at the cost of the Dominion Treasury.

11. That there shall be guaranteed uninterrupted steam communication to Lake Superior within five years, and also the establishment by rail of a connection with the

American railway as soon as it reaches the International line.

12. That the English and French languages be common in the Legislature and Courts, and that all public documents and acts of the Legislature be published in both languages.

13. That the Judge of the Supreme Court speak the French and English languages.

14. That treaties be concluded between the Dominion and the several Indian tribes of the country as soon as possible.

15. That until the population entitles us to more, we have four representatives in the Canadian Parliament— one in the Senate, and three in the Legislative Assembly.

16. That all properties, rights, and privileges, as hitherto enjoyed by us, be respected; and the recognition and arrangement of local custom, usages, and privileges, be made under the control of the Local Legislature.

17. That the Local Legislature of this Territory have full control of all the public land inside a circumference having Fort Garry as the centre, and that the radii of this circumference be the number of miles that the American line is distant from Fort Garry.

18. That every man in this country (except uncivilized and unsettled Indians) who has attained the age of twenty-one years, and every British subject, a stranger to this Territory, who has resided three years in the country, and is a householder, shall have a right to vote at the election of a member to serve in the Legislature of the country, and in the Dominion Parliament; and every foreign subject, other than a British subject, who has resided the same

length of time in the country, and is a householder, shall have the same right to vote, on condition of his taking the oath of allegiance, it being understood that this article be subject to amendment exclusively by the Local Legislature.

19. That the North-West Territory shall never be held liable for any portion of the £300,000 paid to the Hudson's Bay Company, or for any portion of the public debt of Canada, as it stands at the time of our entering the Confederation; and if, thereafter, we be called upon to assume our share of the said public debt, we consent only on condition that we first be allowed the amount for which we shall be held liable.

(Signed)   W. Coldwell,
              Lan. Schmidt,
              Secretaries to the Convention.

APPENDIX B.

LIST OF ARTICLES IN THE BOATS.

IN each boat there will be the following tools and equipment:—Two felling axes, one pickaxe, one spade, one shovel, two hand axes, two Flanders kettles, two frying-pans, two sails, two boathooks, two spare oars (making eight in all), four rowlocks, one set of blocks (single and double), one boat lamp, six thimbles for setting poles, one dipper, one rubber bucket, one boat sponge, two cans of paint (black and white), five pounds of assorted boat nails, one double tin oilcan, one tin with pitch, one tarpaulin, fenders, sixty fathoms tow line, one can mosquito oil, &c., &c., spare plank and tools necessary for repairs. There will also be the cooking utensils, &c., of the boatmen, for which the coxswain of each boat will be responsible. With each brigade of boats there will be a carpenter's chest of tools and a fishing net.

Standing Orders R. R. Expedition.

APPENDIX C.

PROVINCE OF MANITOBA BILL.

AN Act to amend and continue the Act 32 and 33 Victoria, chapter 3, and to establish and provide for the Government of the Province of Manitoba.

Whereas it is probable that Her Majesty the Queen may, pursuant to the "British North America Act, 1867," be pleased to admit Rupert's Land and the North-Western Territory into the Union or Dominion of Canada, before the next session of the Parliament of Canada:

And whereas it is expedient to prepare for the transfer of the said Territories to the Government of Canada at the time appointed by the Queen for such admission:

And whereas it is expedient also to provide for the organization of part of the said Territories as a Province, and for the establishment of a Government thereof, and to make provision for the Civil Government of the remaining part of the said Territories, not included within the limits of the Province:

Therefore, Her Majesty, by and with the advice and consent of the Senate and House of Commons of Canada, enacts as follows:—

1. On, from, and after the day upon which the Queen,

by and with the advice and consent of Her Majesty's Most
Honourable Privy Council, under the authority of the
146th section of the "British North America Act, 1867,"
shall, by Order in Council in that behalf, admit Rupert's
Land and the North-Western Territory into the Union or
Dominion of Canada, there shall be formed out of the
same a Province, which shall be one of the Provinces of
the Dominion of Canada, and which shall be called the
Province of Manitoba, and be bounded as follows : that is
to say, commencing at the point where the meridian of
ninety-six degrees west longitude from Greenwich inter-
sects the parellel of forty-nine degrees north latitude,
thence due west along the said parellel of forty-nine
degrees north latitude (which forms a portion of the
boundary line between the United States of America
and the said North-Western Territory) to the meridian
of ninety-nine degrees of west longitude, then due north
along the said meridian of ninety-nine degrees of west
longitude to the intersection of the same with the parallel
of fifty degrees and thirty minutes north latitude, thence
due east along the said parallel of fifty degrees and thirty
minutes north latitude to its intersection, with the before-
mentioned meridian of ninety-six degrees west longitude—
thence due south along the said meridian of ninety-six
degrees west longitude to the place of beginning.

2. On, from, and after the said day on which the Order
of the Queen in Council shall take effect as aforesaid, the
provisions of the "British North America Act, 1867,"
shall, except those parts thereof which are in terms made,
or by reasonable intendment may be held to be specially
applicable to, or only to affect one or more, but not the

whole of the Provinces now composing the Dominion, and except so far as the same may be varied by this Act, be applicable to the Province of Manitoba, in the same way and to the like extent as they apply to the several Provinces of Canada, and as if the Province of Manitoba had been one of the Provinces originally united by the said Act.

3. The said Province shall be represented in the Senate of Canada by two Members, until it shall have, according to decennial census, a population of fifty thousand souls, and from thenceforth it shall be represented therein by three Members, until it shall have, according to decennial census, a population of seventy-five thousand souls, and from thenceforth it shall be represented therein by four Members.

4. The said Province shall be represented, in the first instance, in the House of Commons, by four Members, and for that purpose shall be divided by proclamation of the Governor-General into four electoral districts, each of which shall be represented by one Member. Provided that on the completion of the census in the year 1881, and of each decennial census afterwards, the representation of the said Province shall be re-adjusted according to the provisions of the fifty-first section of the "British North America Act, 1867."

5. Until the Parliament of Canada otherwise provides, the qualifications of voters at elections of members of the House of Commons shall be the same as for the Legislative Assembly hereinafter mentioned. And no person shall be qualified to be elected or to sit and vote as a member for any electoral district, unless he is a duly qualified voter within the said Province.

6. For the said Province there shall be an officer styled the Lieutenant-Governor, appointed by the Governor-General in Council, by instrument, under the Great Seal of Canada.

7. The Executive Council of the Province shall be composed of such persons and under such designations as the Lieutenant-Governor shall from time to time think fit, and in the first instance of not more than five persons.

8. Unless and until the Executive Government of the Province otherwise directs, the seat of Government of the same shall be at Fort Garry, or within one mile thereof.

9. There shall be a Legislature for the Province, consisting of the Lieutenant-Governor, and of two Houses, styled respectively the Legislative Council of Manitoba, and the Legislative Assembly of Manitoba.

10. The Legislative Council shall, in the first instance, be composed of seven Members, and after the expiration of four years from the time of the first appointment of such seven Members, may be increased to not more than twelve Members. Every Member of the Legislative Council shall be appointed by the Lieutenant-Governor in the Queen's name, by instrument, under the Great Seal of Manitoba, and shall hold office for the term of his life, unless and until the Legislature of Manitoba otherwise provides under the " British North America Act, 1867."

11. The Lieutenant-Governor may from time to time, by instrument under the Great Seal, appoint a Member of the Legislative Council to be Speaker thereof, and may remove him, and appoint another in his stead.

12. Until the Legislature of the Province otherwise

provides, the presence of a majority of the whole number of the Legislative Council, including the Speaker, shall be necessary to constitute a meeting for the exercise of its powers.

13. Questions arising in the Legislative Council shall be decided by a majority of voices, and the Speaker shall in all cases have a vote, and when voices are equal, the decision shall be deemed to be in the negative.

14. The Legislative Assembly shall be composed of twenty-four Members, to be elected to represent the electoral divisions into which the said Province may be divided by the Lieutenant-Governor as hereinafter mentioned.

15. The presence of a majority of the Members of the Legislative Assembly shall be necessary to constitute a meeting of the House for the exercise of its powers, and for that purpose the Speaker shall be reckoned as a Member.

16. The Lieutenant-Governor shall (within six months of the date of the Order of Her Majesty in Council admitting Rupert's Land and the North-Western Territory into the Union), by Proclamation under the Great Seal, divide the said Province into twenty-four electoral divisions, due regard being had to existing local divisions and population.

17. Every male person shall be entitled to vote for a member to serve in the Legislative Assembly for any electoral division, who is qualified as follows; that is to say, if he is—

    (1.) Of the full age of twenty-one years, and not subject to any legal incapacity.

(2.) A subject of Her Majesty by birth or naturalization.

(3.) And a *bonâ fide* householder within the electoral division, at the date of the Writ of
Election of the same, and has been a *bonâ
fide* householder for one year next before the
said date ; or,

(4.) If, being of the full age of twenty-one years,
and not subject to any incapacity, and a subject
of Her Majesty by birth or naturalization, he
was any time within twelve months prior to the
passing of this Act, and (though in the interim
temporarily absent) is at the time of such
election a *bonâ fide* householder, and was
resident within the electoral division at the
date of the Writ of Election for the same.

But this fourth sub-section shall apply only to the first
election to be held under this Act for Members to serve in
the Legislative Assembly aforesaid.

18. For the first election of Members to serve in the
Legislative Assemby, and until the Legislature of the
Province otherwise provides, the Lieutenant-Governor shall
cause writs to be issued by such person, in such form, and
addressed to such Returning Officers as he thinks fit ; and
for such first election, and until the Legislature of the
Province otherwise provides, the Lieutenant-Governor
shall, by Proclamation, prescribe and declare the oaths to
be taken by voters, the powers and duties of Returning
and Deputy Returning Officers, the proceedings to be
observed at such elections, and the period during
which such election may be continued, and such other

provisions in respect to such first election as he may think fit.

19. Every Legislative Assembly shall continue for four years from the date of the return of the Writs for returning the same (subject, nevertheless, to being sooner dissolved by the Lieutenant-Governor), and no longer, and the first session thereof shall be called at such time as the Lieutenant-Governor shall appoint.

20. There shall be a session of the Legislature once at least in every year, so that twelve months shall not intervene between the last sitting of the last Legislature in one session, and its first sitting in the next session.

21. The following provisions of the "British North America Act, 1867," respecting the House of Commons of Canada, shall extend and apply to the Legislative Assembly, that is to say:—Provisions relating to the election of a Speaker, originally, and on vacancies—the duties of the Speaker—the absence of the Speaker and the mode of voting, as if those provisions were here re-enacted, and made applicable in terms to the Legislative Assembly.

22. In and for the Province, the said Legislature may exclusively make laws in relation to education, subject and according to the following provisions :—

    (1.) Nothing in any such law shall prejudicially affect any right or privilege with respect to Denominational Schools which any class of persons have by law or practice in the Province at the Union.

    (2.) An appeal shall lie to the Governor-General in Council from any act or decision of the Legis-

lature of the Province, or of any provisional
authority, affecting any right or privilege of
the Protestant or Roman Catholic minority of
the Queen's subjects in relation to education.

(3.) In case any such Provisional Law as from time
to time seems to the Governor-General in
Council requisite for the due execution of the
provisions of this section is not made, or in
case any decision of the Governor-General in
Council on any appeal under this section is
not duly executed by the proper provincial
authority in that behalf, then, and in every
such case, and as far only as the circumstances
of each case require, the Parliament of Canada
may make remedial laws for the due execution
of the provisions of this section, and of any
decision of the Governor-General in Council
under this section.

23. Either the English or the French language may be
used by any person in the debates of the Houses of the
Legislature, and both these languages shall be used in the
respective Records and Journals of those Houses, and
either of those languages may be used by any person, or
in Pleading or Process, in or issuing from any Court in
Canada established under the "British North America Act,
1867," or in or from all or any of the Courts of the Province.   The Acts of the Legislature shall be printed and
published in both those languages.

24. Inasmuch as the Province is not in debt, the said
Province shall be entitled to be paid, and to receive from
the Government of Canada, by half-yearly payments in

advance, interest at the rate of five per centum per annum on the sum of four hundred and seventy-two thousand and ninety dollars.

25. The sum of thirty thousand dollars shall be paid yearly by Canada to the Province for the support of its Government and Legislature, and an annual grant in aid of the said Province shall be made, equal to eighty cents per head of the population, estimated at seventeen thousand souls; and such grant of eighty cents per head shall be augmented in proportion to the increase of population, as may be shown by the census that shall be taken thereof in the year One Thousand Eight Hundred and Eighty-one, and by each subsequent decennial census, until its population amounts to four hundred thousand souls, at which amount such grant shall remain thereafter, and such sum shall be in full settlement of all future demands on Canada, and shall be paid half-yearly, in advance, to the said Province.

26. Canada will assume and defray the charges for the following services :—

    (1.) Salary of the Lieutenant-Governor.

    (2.) Salaries and allowances of the Judges of the Superior and District or County Courts.

    (3.) Charges in respect of the Department of the Customs.

    (4.) Postal Department.

    (5.) Protection of Fisheries.

    (6.) Militia.

    (7.) Geological Survey.

    (8.) The Penitentiary.

(9.) And such further charges as may be incident to and connected with the services which by the " British North America Act, 1867," appertain to the General Government, and as are, or may be, allowed to the other Provinces.

27. The Customs' duties now by law chargeable in Rupert's Land, shall be continued without increase for the period of three years from and after the passing of this Act, and the proceeds of such duties shall form part of the Consolidated Revenue Fund of Canada.

28. Such provisions of the Customs' Laws of Canada (other than such as prescribe the rate of duties payable) as may from time to time be declared by the Governor-General in Council to apply to the Province of Manitoba, shall be applicable thereto, and be in force therein accordingly.

29. Such provisions of the Laws of Canada respecting the Inland Revenue, including those fixing the amount of duties, as may be from time to time declared by the Governor-General in Council applicable to the said Province, shall apply thereto, and be in force accordingly.

30. All ungranted or waste lands in the Province shall be, from and after the date of the said transfer, vested in the Crown, and administered by the Government of Canada for the purposes of the Dominion, subject to and except and so far as the same may be affected by the conditions and stipulations contained in the agreement for the surrender of Rupert's Land by the Hudson's Bay Company to Her Majesty.

31. And whereas it is expedient, towards the extinguishment of the Indian Title to the lands in the Province, to

appropriate a portion of such ungranted lands to the extent of one million four hundred thousand acres thereof for the benefit of the families of the half-breed residents, it is hereby enacted that, under regulations to be from time to time made by the Governor-General in Council, the Lieutenant-Governor shall select such lots or tracts in such parts of the Province as he may deem expedient, to the extent aforesaid, and divide the same among the children of the half-breed heads of families residing in the Province at the time of the said transfer to Canada, and the same shall be granted to the said children respectively, in such mode and on such conditions as to settlement or otherwise as the Governor-General in Council shall from time to time determine.

32. For the quieting of titles and assuring the settlers in the Province the peaceable possession of lands now held by them, it is enacted as follows :—

> (1.) All grants of land in freehold made by the Hudson's Bay Company, up to the eighth day of March, in the year 1869, shall, if required by the owner, be confirmed by grant from the Crown.

> (2.) All grants of estates less than freehold in land made by the Hudson's Bay Company up to the eighth day of March aforesaid, shall, if required by the owner, be converted into an estate in freehold by grant from the Crown.

> (3.) All titles by occupancy with the sanction and under the licence and authority of the Hudson's Bay Company up to the eighth day of March aforesaid, of land in that part of the

Province in which the Indian Title has been extinguished, shall, if required by the owner, be converted into an estate in freehold by grant from the Crown.

(4.) All persons in peaceable possession of tracts of land at the time of the transfer to Canada, in those parts of the Province in which the Indian Title has not been extinguished, shall have the right of pre-emption of the same, on such terms and conditions as may be determined by the Governor in Council.

(5.) The Lieutenant-Governor is hereby authorized, under regulations to be made from time to time by the Governor-General in Council, to make all such provisions for ascertaining and adjusting, on fair and equitable terms, the rights of common, and rights of cutting hay, held and enjoyed by the settlers in the Province, and for the commutation of the same by grants of land from the Crown.

33. The Governor-General in Council shall from time to time settle and appoint the mode and form of Grants of Land from the Crown, and any Order in Council for that purpose, when published in the *Canada Gazette*, shall have the same force and effect as if it were a portion of this Act.

34. Nothing in this Act shall in any way prejudice or affect the rights or properties of the Hudson's Bay Company, as contained in the conditions under which that company surrendered Rupert's Land to Her Majesty.

35. And with respect to such portion of Rupert's Land

s

and the North-Western Territory, as is not included in the Province of Manitoba, it is hereby enacted, that the Lieutenant-Governor of the said Province shall be appointed, by commission under the Great Seal of Canada, to be the Lieutenant-Governor of the same, under the name of the North-West Territories, and subject to the provisions of the Act in the next section mentioned.

36. Except as hereinbefore is enacted and provided, the Act of the Parliament of Canada passed in the now last Session thereof, and entitled "An Act for the temporary government of Rupert's Land, and the North-Western Territory when united to Canada," is hereby re-enacted, extended, and continued in force until the first day of January, 1871, and until the end of the Session of Parliament then next succeeding.

　　　　True copy.　　　(Signed)　　　JOHN F. TAYLOR,
　　　　　　　　　　　　　　　　　　　　　　　　　　　Clerk of the Senate.

OFFICE OF THE SENATE OF CANADA,
　　OTTAWA, 16TH MAY, 1870.

EMBARKATION RETURN, Red River Expeditionary Force, from McNeill Bay, Lake Shebandowan.

Departure Date	Departure Hour	Brigade	Number of boats	Officer Commanding	Regiment Embarked	Numbers Officers	N.C.O. and Men	Voyageurs	Guides	Total	Biscuits brls.	Flour brls.	Pork brls.	Sugar brls.	Tea chs.	Beans bgs.	Preserved potatoes case	Pepper lb.	Days' rations, for total	Ammunition, rounds	Augurs	Axes Felling	Pick	Blankets	Pans	Chisels case
1. July 16th	8.30 P.M.	A	6	Capt. Young	1st Bn. 60th	5	50	12	1	68	34	20	45	6	6	8	6	8½	5,000	...	10	5	...	case	...
2. „ „	„	B	6	„ Ward	„	4	50	12	...	66	28	31	42	6	6	10	8	8	6,000	...	10	5	...	...	...
3. „ „	„	C	5	Lieut. Alleyne, R.A.	R.A. and R.E.	2	38	10	...	50	21	17	25	4th	3rd	4	8	5	...	2	12	16	...	1	2
4. „ 17th	3 P.M.	D	7	Capt. Dundas	1st Bn. 60th	4	50	14	1	69	37	31	52	8	7	14	8	9	6,000	...	12	6	...	...	...
5. „ „	4 „	E	6	„ Buller	„	3	50	12	...	65	50	32	42	6	5	9	8	8	5,000	...	10	5	...	...	...
6. „ 18th	6 „	F	6	„ Northey	„	3	49	12	1	65	50½	37	44	6	6	13	8	8	5,000	1	10	5	25	...	2
7. „ 19th	4.30 P.M.	G	7	„ Wallace	1st Bn. 60th A.S.C. and A.H.C.	5	58	14	1	78	40	42	50	7	7	13	8	9	6,000	...	19	13	...	...	...
8. „ 21st	8 A.M.	H	6	„ Calderon	1st. Bn. 60th	4	49	12	1	66	51	33	44	6	6	11	8	8	5,000	...	10	5	...	...	...
9. „ „	4 P.M.	I	6	„ Scott	1st Ontario Rifles	6	48	12	1	67	54	35	46	7	6	10	9	8	5,000	...	10	5	...	...	...
10. „ „	6 „	Gig	1	„ Huyshe, 1st R. B.	H. Q. Staff	2	4	2	...	8	2	2	3	36	18	...	1	4	...	...	2	1	...	...	...
11. „ 22nd	12.30 P.M.	K	6	„ McDonald	1st Ontario Rifles	4	49	12	...	65	*49	37	45	6	6	10	11	8	5,000	...	10	5	...	...	...
12. „ „	3.30 „	L	6	„ Herchmer	„ „	3	48	12	1	64	†60	37	44	8	6	9	9	8	5,000	...	10	5	...	...	...
						45	543	136	7	731	476½ 354	482	70 47 H 28 H	64	111	92	88	...	53,000	3	125	74	25	1	4

* 47 at 48 lbs.
2 at 60 „

CAMP, LAKE SHEBANDOWAN, 23rd *July*, 1870.

Hammers, small.	Hatchets, hand.	Kettles, Flanders.	Ovens, Field.	Pans, Frying.	Bedding, Hp., bags of.	Powder kegs.	Rope lashings.	Rope, Manilla coil.	Saws + out.	Saws, hand.	Scales and weights.	Shovels.	Spades.	Spikes and nails.	Tapes, measuring.	Tarpaulins.	Tents, bell.	Marquees.	Slings, rope.		Strops, portage.	Bags, spare.	Tins of mosquito oil.	Bags, waterprf.		Medical comforts and equipment, boxes.	Tins.	Canteens, Hp., A. and B.	Linseed meal, boxes.	Salt, kegs.	Stones, grind.	Tobacco, boxes.	Soap, cases of.	Number of days' rations for total 781 men.	
																			Large.	Small.				For blankets.	For accoutrements.										
...	11	10	...	7	...	...	coils ...	...	...	...	...	5	5	lb. ...	...	...	6	...	15	20	36	56	6	10	5	...	30	...	...	...	...	...	...	Biscuit ... 54	} 85
...	10	10	...	7	...	...	...	...	...	...	...	5	5	...	...	...	7	...	15	20	30	56	6	10	5	...	33	...	...	...	...	...	...	Flour ... 31	
1	10	8	...	6	...	2	1	1	...	...	...	8	4	50	1	...	6	...	12	16	24	39	5	8	5	...	15	...	...	...	1	...	...	Pork 66	
...	12	12	...	8	...	...	...	...	4	...	6	6	...	...	...	8	...	18	24	36	81	7	12	6	...	34	...	...	...	...	...	...	...	Sugar 71	
...	10	10	...	7	...	...	...	...	...	5	5	...	...	...	6	...	15	20	30	99	6	10	5	...	27	...	...	...	...	...	...	...	...	Tea... 69	
2	10	15	...	7	...	...	...	2	3	...	5	5	...	...	...	15	...	15	20	30	73	6	10	5	...	23	...	...	...	...	...	...	Beans ... 43	} 71
...	22	13	1	16	...	...	...	...	1	13	13	...	...	...	11	...	18	24	36	76	7	12	6	13	32	2	1	1	...	4	...	Potatoes... 28	
...	10	10	...	7	8	...	...	5	1	...	5	5	...	...	...	6	...	15	20	30	67	6	10	5	13	31	...	1	...	...	...	...	Pepper 69	
...	19	10	...	7	...	...	...	...	...	...	5	5	...	...	...	6	...	15	20	30	69	6	10	5	7	26	...	...	...	4	...	...		
...	2	1	...	1	...	...	...	...	...	...	...	1	...	...	...	2	...	...	6	4	1	...	...	...	4	...	...	...	...	...	...		
...	10	8	...	7	...	...	...	...	...	...	5	5	...	...	...	5	...	15	20	33	60	6	10	5	3	27	...	...	...	...	...	...		
...	10	6	...	7	...	...	...	...	...	...	5	5	...	...	...	6	...	15	20	30	60	6	10	5	...	26	...	...	...	...	1	1		
3	127	113	1	89	8	2	1	1	7	8	1	67	64	50	1	...	84	...	168	234	348	660	68	112	57	41	313	2	2	1	1	9	1		

+ 53 at 84 lbs.
  1 at 60 „
  6 at 42 „

(Signed)   A. MEYER,
Deputy Assistant Commissary-General.

APPENDIX E.

STANDING ORDERS FOR THE RED RIVER EXPEDITIONARY FORCE.

TORONTO, 14TH MAY, 1870.

1. THE Expeditionary Force will proceed from the end of the Thunder Bay Road to the Lake of the Woods in boats. It will move by detachments, consisting of one or more companies. To each company a brigade of five boats will be attached.

2. The boats will be numbered 1, 2, 3, &c., &c., and the brigade will be distinguished by letters beginning at A.

3. In each boat there will be the following tools and equipment:—Two felling axes, one pickaxe, one spade, one shovel, two hand axes, two Flanders kettles, two frying pans, two sails, two boathooks, two spare oars (making eight in all), four rowlocks, one set of blocks (single and double), one boat lamp, six thimbles for setting poles, one dipper, one rubber bucket, one boat sponge, two cans of paint (black and white), five lbs. assorted boat nails, one double tin oilcan, one tin with pitch, one tarpaulin,

s 2

fenders, sixty fathoms tow line, one can mosquito oil, &c., &c., spare plank, and tools necessary for repairs. There will also be the cooking utensils, &c., of the boatmen, for which the coxswain of each boat will be responsible. In every boat there will be thirty days' rations for the soldiers and boatmen, besides, also, about one ton of surplus stores.

4. With each brigade of boats there will be a carpenter's chest of tools and a fishing net.

5. The scale of rations for every one will be as follows : 1 lb. of biscuit, or $1\frac{1}{2}$ lbs. of soft bread, 1 lb. of salt pork, or $1\frac{1}{4}$ lbs. of fresh meat, 2 ozs. of sugar, 1 oz. of tea, $\frac{1}{2}$ oz. of salt when fresh meat is issued, $\frac{1}{3}$ pint of beans or $\frac{1}{4}$ lb. preserved potatoes, $\frac{1}{36}$ oz. pepper ; the ration of flour when issued to be $1\frac{1}{2}$ lbs.

6. In each boat there will be three voyageurs, one of whom will be the coxswain, and have entire charge of managing the boat.

7. The Officer or N. C. Officer in command of the men in each boat will render him every assistance in doing so, and any one going counter to his advice must understand that he is taking on himself a grave responsibility, which may possibly affect the safety of the whole party.

8. No one, under any pretence, will be allowed to sit on the gunwale of the boats, and all must learn to sit steadily, moving as little as possible when the boat is under weigh, particularly in rapid water. When under sail the sheets must never be made fast; they must invariably be held by the hand.

9. To prevent supplies being sent to wrong places, it must be remembered that all stores belonging to the

Expedition have been divided into three classes, X, Y, Z, and marked accordingly; those marked Z are to be taken with the force when it finally starts from Fort Frances; those marked Y are to be left at Fort Frances, and those marked X at Fort William.

10. Officers commanding companies will not allow, under any pretence whatever, any person not belonging to the force to be carried in the boats, unless he has a written permission, signed by the Officer commanding the force, or by Lieutenant-Colonel Bolton.

11. The Officer in immediate command at the Shebandowan end of the road will be held strictly responsible that no unauthorised person embarks. He will attend at the departure of each brigade of boats to see this order rigidly carried out.

12. Detachments will be posted temporarily at various portages along the route, for the purpose of facilitating the transport of supplies to Fort Frances.

13. They will carry out this duty as follows :—They will daily send back to the nearest portage in rear a sufficient number of boats to carry fifteen tons of stores : all the boatmen to be employed on this service, supplemented by as many soldiers as the Officer commanding on the spot may consider necessary; all soldiers to take their arms and accoutrements with them.

14. One Officer will invariably accompany the boats on this duty, and will take with him at each trip supplies sufficient for the crews for three days, together with a portion of tools, &c., &c. The remainder of the detachment to be employed daily in carrying over the portage at their post the fifteen tons of stores brought up by the

boats on the previous day, and loading them in the boats sent back to receive them by the detachment in front.

15. The day after each detachment has reached its position, it will commence operations by sending back for the surplus stores of the detachment in rear. This will be continued daily, until all the reserve supplies for Fort Frances have been sent forward.

16. The greatest possible care will be necessary in loading and unloading the boats, to guard against their being injured. The Indian voyageurs having had great experience in loading canoes, their advice is to be attended to in this matter.

17. Every one concerned must learn that the success of the undertaking depends upon these boats, and if those provided be rendered unserviceable they cannot be replaced.

18. The Colonel commanding will therefore have no alternative but to leave behind the crews of any boats that are rendered unfit for use.

19. Colonel McNeill will be stationed at the Shebandowan end of the road. Special instructions will be issued to him for his guidance.

20. Mr. Meyer will be the Control Officer there, to superintend the shipment of stores. He will be responsible for the loading of the boats, and will decide also the description and amount of stores to be sent with each, in addition to those laid down as forming the equipment of each boat. He will hand over to the Captain of each company, the evening before he starts, the complete equipment of his brigade of boats, receiving a receipt from him for it. The Officer commanding the company

will make an exact copy of the list in his pocket-book, specifying how he has distributed the stores, &c., by boats, and the name of the Officer or sergeant in charge of each boat.

Mr. Meyer will also hand over to every Officer commanding a company rations complete for his men and voyageurs for thirty days, taking a receipt for the same ; a list of these provisions to be also entered by the Captain in his pocket-book. These provisions must be distributed throughout the boats, so that in each boat there will be thirty days' rations for every one in it.

21. Mr. Meyer will also hand over to every Officer commanding a company, as much surplus supplies (about 2,000 lbs. weight for each boat) as his boats can conveniently carry—Mr. Meyer to be the judge on this point— giving him an accurate list of the articles, which will be sent on with the stores when they are passed forward beyond the portage where the company is to be temporarily stationed on the line of route.   This list will be signed as correct, or otherwise, by all the Officers commanding at the several portages when the stores pass through their posts ; any article deficient to be noted on the list.

22. After the last detachment has left, the stores noted in the margin[1] will be shipped with as little delay as possible, at the rate of fifteen tons a day.   One, or, if possible, two days before the last fifteen tons are to be dispatched from Shebandowan Lake, Colonel McNeill will notify in

[1] Barrels of flour, barrels of pork, barrels of sugar, bags of biscuit, bags of salt, bags of beans, tins of potatoes, tins of pepper, chests of tea.

writing, to all the posts in advance, stating when the last of the reserved stores will be sent through. He will send a written memorandum with the last fifteen tons, saying they are the last.

Upon the receipt of this information (which will be signed by the Officer commanding each detachment, and forwarded on to the next post), Officers commanding at all posts on the line between Shebandowan and Fort Frances will proceed without delay to the latter place, taking on with them their boats and all their equipments, and the remains of the thirty days' provisions sent originally with them.

23. Upon reaching Fort Frances they will complete their boats with thirty days' rations for all persons with them, and will embark all their surplus stores as the Control Officer, Mr. Mellish, may indicate.

24. As soon as the detachment left at Bare Portage reaches Fort Frances, the 200 men of the 1st, 60th Rifles, which had been stationed there during this movement, will start for Rat Portage to work at it.

25. By these arrangements, the last detachment that left Shebandowan Lake will reach Fort Frances the day after the last fifteen tons of the reserve supplies to be stored there reach that place.

26. The detachments from Fort Frances will severally start from thence, as soon as relieved by the detachment coming up in rear.

27. Fresh instructions will be issued at Fort Frances with reference to the forward movement from that place.

28. In case of a man falling seriously ill or being seriously injured whilst the troops are moving to their

several stations, the medical officer with the detachment will decide whether the illness or injury is of such a nature as to prevent the man from proceeding further. If he pronounces the man as likely to be unfit for work for some time to come, he is to be left behind at the nearest portage where a detachment is to be stationed, in charge of a non-commissioned officer and one man, who will take their arms, accoutrements, &c., &c., with them. A week's provisions to be left for the three men. All Officers commanding detachments passing by them to see that they have always that quantity in their possession.

As soon as the detachment to be stationed at the portage where the sick man has been left arrives, he will be sent with the returning boats to the rear, to be forwarded on to the Hospital at Fort William.

If there is no medical officer with the detachment, the sick man will be left behind in a similar manner until the arrival of a detachment having a doctor with it.

In both cases the N. C. officer and private left with the man will proceed on to join their company as soon as the man has been sent to the rear.

The Officer commanding the 12th detachment, whilst *en route* between his post at the Kashaboiwe Portage and Fort Frances, will use his own discretion as to whether he will send serious cases of illness to the Hospital at Fort William, or take them on with him to Fort Frances. If he can possibly do so, he should send them to the former place.

29. Officers commanding detachments, from the time of their embarking at Shebandowan, will keep a Journal of their route, entering the exact hour they start each morn-

ing, the hours they halt for meals and start again, the
time they reach the halting-place for the night, giving the
name of the place, the state of the weather, whether they
used oars or sails during the day, &c., &c.   All irregu-
larities committed by their men to be recorded.   They
will also state whether they found the fires made by the
previous detachment still burning or not.

30. The Officers commanding the several detachments
posted at the portages will encamp their men in as com-
pact order as possible on the end of the portage nearest
to Fort Frances, except when, from the marshiness of the
ground, or other peculiar causes, there are good reasons
for departing from this order.

They will pile up their provisions close to the landing
place at the Fort Frances side of the portage, covering
them over with the boat tarpaulins, and doing everything
in their power to protect them from the weather.

The boats will remain on the Shebandowan side of the
portage, every precaution being taken to secure them at
night by their painters to the shore. When there is a good
beach they should be hauled up for the night, being
launched every morning.

31. Each detachment will have a guard, consisting of
at least three men per company.   They will mount with
arms and accoutrements.   Up to Fort Frances the arms
for the other men will remain in their arm chest, unless
when for special reasons the Officers commanding detachments may consider it necessary for the men to keep their
arms in the tents.

The arms, if kept in these arm chests, must be frequently inspected by the Captains of Companies, to see

that they are free from rust, and in good and serviceable order.

32. The greatest possible precautions to be taken to guard against the woods being set on fire.

The cooking places will be established as near the water as possible, and no other fires are to be allowed in the camp without the express permission of the Officer commanding the detachment, who will assure himself, before giving such permission, that there is no danger to be apprehended.

When on the move, Officers commanding companies will be held responsible that all fires are extinguished previous to their leaving a camp.

33. As a rule, the reveille will sound at 3 A.M. every morning, and the boats will start as soon after that as possible, the men to have some hot tea before starting. The boats of each brigade must keep as near together as possible, the Captain, with his bugler, being in the leading boat, the senior subaltern and a sergeant in the rear boat.

A halt of one hour will be made at 8 A.M., for breakfast; another halt of an hour at 1 P.M. for dinner. Officers commanding companies may, of course, depart a little from these hours for meals; but, under no circumstances, is more than an hour to be allowed for each meal. They will always halt for the night at least one full hour before dark, so that there will be ample time to establish the camp for the night. When on the move, it is not advisable to pitch tents except when it rains or threatens to do so; even then, the smallest possible number should be pitched.

34. When it is necessary to track the boats, the crew will be divided into two parties, each consisting of four or five soldiers and one voyageur. Sergeants are not to be employed in tracking. These two parties to relieve one another every two hours. Officers and N. C. Officers in charge of boats will see that the men returning to their boats after tracking put on their serge frocks at once, which are not to be removed for at least half an hour afterwards.

All Officers belonging to this force will be most careful in impressing upon those under their command the great necessity there is for cultivating the good-will of the Indians and others employed as voyageurs.

Colonel Wolseley will punish with the utmost severity any one who ill-treats them.

The same rule applies to all Indians who may be met on the line of route.

It must be remembered that the Government has made a treaty with them, securing the right of way through their country ; all are therefore bound to protect them from injury, and it is of special importance that our intercourse with them should be of the most friendly nature.

No Indians but those actually attached to the force are to be allowed to pass the night in our camps.

(Signed)   G. J. WOLSELEY,

Colonel Commanding Expeditionary Force.

APPENDIX F.

DAILY RATION OF FOOD FOR RED RIVER EXPE-DITIONARY FORCE.

1 lb. of salt pork, or $1\frac{1}{2}$ lb. of fresh meat.
1 lb. of biscuit, or $1\frac{1}{2}$ lb. of fresh bread.
$\frac{1}{8}$ pint of beans, or $\frac{1}{4}$ lb. of preserved potatoes.
1 oz. of tea, 2 ozs. of sugar.
$\frac{1}{2}$ oz. salt when fresh meat is issued.
$\frac{1}{36}$ oz. pepper.

CLOTHING ADOPTED FOR THE RED RIVER EXPE-DITIONARY FORCE.

Worn on the Person.	*In the Pack.*
1 flannel shirt.	1 flannel shirt.
1 pair woollen socks.	2 pairs woollen socks.
1 pair buff mocassins.	1 pair ammunition boots.
1 forage cap, with peak and cover.	1 thick woollen night-cap.
1 serge frock (with pockets).	1 tunic.
1 pair serge trousers.	1 pair cloth trousers.
1 haversack.	1 towel.
1 clasp knife.	1 piece of soap.
1 tin cup.	1 brush (clothes or boot).
1 waist belt.	1 comb, 1 linen bandage.
1 mess tin } on pack.	1 small book, 1 housewife.
1 great coat }	Knife, fork, and spoon.

INDEX.

A.

ABYSSINIAN WAR, its difficulties and cost compared with those of the Red River Expedition, 236.

Archibald, Hon. Mr., appointed Lieutenant-Governor of Red River Settlement, 36; his arrival at the Settlement, 203, 218; his difficulties and prospects, 212, 234; his recognition of the success of the expedition, 235.

B.

BARIL LAKE and portage, 120.

Baptiste, an Iroquois voyageur, his skill and energy, 156, 175.

"Bill of Rights" issued by the insurgents, 11, 14; Appendix A, 241.

Black flies, 82.

"Blazing" trees, to mark the route, 126.

Blue-berries, their abundance, 134.

"Boat Transport Service," its organization, 22; Mr. S. J. Dawson engaged by Government, boats described, boatmen or "voyageurs," 29, 30; Appendix B, 245; first boats sent on from Thunder Bay, 59; Col. Wolseley determines to send boats up the Kaministiquia river, 66; difficulty of carrying boats over "portages," 69, 70; Shebandowan, 97; voyage across the lake, 103; mode of carrying boats over portages, 110; dangers from the rapids, 131; descent of the Winnipeg river, 172-183.

Bolton, Lieut.-Col., his exertions during the expedition, 33, 42, 200, 204.

Boulton, Major, opposes the insurgents, 15; captured by Riel and sentenced to death, 16.

Bruce, John, President of insurgent Provisional Government, 5.

Buffalo hunting in the "far west," 229.

Butler, Lieut., his mission to Lake Superior, visit to Fort Garry, joins Col. Wolseley, 141; his exertions in the expedition, 169, 189, 192.

C.

CAMBRIDGE, H.R.H. the Duke of, General Order on the success of the expedition, 205.

Canada, acquires the territorial rights of the Hudson's Bay Company over the Red River Settlement, 3; Commissioners sent to Red River, 11; excitement on hearing the execution of Scott, 20; Government arrangements for transport of expedition to Thunder Bay, 31; duty of Government to provide railway communication to Red River, 210.

Canoes, Indian, their fragility, lightness, and safety, 181.

Cartier, Sir George, French Canadian Minister in the Dominion Government, his influence in the Cabinet, 36; his policy conducive to the insurrection, his supposed complicity, 212, 216, 217.

Chippewa Indians, their language, customs, wigwams, burials, &c., "Crooked Neck," an old chief, 143-152.

T

* 9 7 8 1 8 4 7 3 4 4 4 5 8 *